AF278393

West Virginia Legal Research

CAROLINA ACADEMIC PRESS
LEGAL RESEARCH SERIES

Tenielle Fordyce-Ruff, Series Editor
Suzanne E. Rowe, Series Editor Emerita

❧

Arizona, Third Edition — Tamara S. Herrera

Arkansas, Second Edition — Coleen M. Barger, Cheryl L. Reinhart &
Cathy L. Underwood

California, Third Edition — Aimee Dudovitz, Hether C. Macfarlane, & Suzanne E. Rowe

Colorado, Second Edition — Robert Michael Linz

Connecticut — Jessica G. Hynes

Federal, Second Edition — Mary Garvey Algero, Spencer L. Simons,
Suzanne E. Rowe, Scott Childs & Sarah E. Ricks

Florida, Fourth Edition — Barbara J. Busharis, Jennifer LaVia & Suzanne E. Rowe

Georgia — Nancy P. Johnson, Elizabeth G. Adelman & Nancy J. Adams

Idaho, Second Edition — Tenielle Fordyce-Ruff & Kristina J. Running

Illinois, Second Edition — Mark E. Wojcik

Iowa, Second Edition — John D. Edwards, Karen L. Wallace & Melissa H. Weresh

Kansas — Joseph A. Custer & Christopher L. Steadham

Kentucky, Second Edition — William A. Hilyerd, Kurt X. Metzmeier & David J. Ensign

Louisiana, Third Edition — Mary Garvey Algero

Massachusetts, Second Edition — E. Joan Blum & Shaun B. Spencer

Michigan, Third Edition — Pamela Lysaght & Cristina D. Lockwood

Minnesota — Suzanne Thorpe

Mississippi — Kristy L. Gilliland

Missouri, Third Edition — Wanda M. Temm & Julie M. Cheslik

New York, Third Edition — Elizabeth G. Adelman, Theodora Belniak,
Courtney L. Selby & Brian Detweiler

North Carolina, Second Edition — Scott Childs & Sara Sampson

North Dakota — Anne Mullins & Tammy Pettinato

Ohio, Second Edition — Sara Sampson, Katherine L. Hall & Carolyn Broering-Jacobs

Oklahoma — Darin K. Fox, Darla W. Jackson & Courtney L. Selby

Oregon, Fourth Edition — Suzanne E. Rowe & Megan Austin

Pennsylvania, Second Edition — Barbara J. Busharis, Catherine M. Dunn,
Bonny L. Tavares & Carla P. Wale

Tennessee, Second Edition — Scott Childs, Sibyl Marshall & Carol McCrehan Parker

Texas, Second Edition — Spencer L. Simons

Washington, Second Edition — Julie Heintz-Cho, Tom Cobb & Mary A. Hotchkiss

West Virginia, Second Edition — Hollee Schwartz Temple

Wisconsin — Patricia Cervenka & Leslie Behroozi

Wyoming, Second Edition — Debora A. Person & Tawnya K. Plumb

❧

West Virginia Legal Research

Second Edition

Hollee Schwartz Temple

Tenielle Fordyce-Ruff, Series Editor
Suzanne E. Rowe, Series Editor Emerita

Carolina Academic Press
Durham, North Carolina

Copyright © 2018
Hollee Schwartz Temple
All Rights Reserved.

Library of Congress Cataloging-in-Publication Data

Names: Temple, Hollee Schwartz, author.
Title: West Virginia legal research / by Hollee Schwartz Temple.
Description: Second edition. | Durham, North Carolina : Carolina
    Academic Press, LLC, [2018] | Series: Legal research series | Includes
    bibliographical references and index.
Identifiers: LCCN 2018030259 | ISBN 9781531012687 (alk. paper)
Subjects: LCSH: Legal research--West Virginia.
Classification: LCC KFW1275 .T46 2018 | DDC 340.072/0753--dc23
LC record available at https://lccn.loc.gov/2018030259

CAROLINA ACADEMIC PRESS, LLC

700 Kent Street
Durham, North Carolina 27701
Telephone (919) 489-7486
Fax (919) 493-5668
www.cap-press.com

Printed in the United States of America
2019 Printing

For the inspiring students
of West Virginia University College of Law
past, present, and future

Summary of Contents

Contents

List of Tables and Figures

Tables

Figures

Series Note

The Legal Research Series published by Carolina Academic Press includes titles from many states around the country as well as a separate text on federal legal research. The goal of each book is to provide law students, practitioners, paralegals, college students, laypeople, and librarians with the essential elements of legal research in each jurisdiction. Unlike more bibliographic texts, the Legal Research Series books seek to explain concisely both the sources of legal research and the process for conducting legal research effectively.

Preface and Acknowledgments

I wrote this book because West Virginia matters. Though I was not born in this state, I have grown to love it over the last 15 years of teaching at West Virginia University College of Law. I didn't want the Carolina Academic Press series on state law research to be missing a title devoted to the legal research process in West Virginia, my adopted "home among the hills."

This book is intended to benefit a broad audience. I hope law students and other novice researchers will benefit from its detailed explanation of the research process. I hope experienced researchers will enjoy a text that pulls together the best of print and online sources available for West Virginia legal research. I hope citizens of the state who are seeking to conduct research on their own will find what they need in this concise guide.

I owe thanks to many people who encouraged me in both the original endeavor and the second edition. First, I am grateful to editors Suzanne Rowe and Tenielle Fordyce-Ruff. Next, thank you to the many student research assistants who provided support, including Julie Preusch, Alan Wilson, Lauren Rose Givhan, Ryan Loos, and Bryce Schuman.

Our library staff is top notch. Thanks especially to Mark Podvia for helping me update the text. Thanks also to the Legal Writing team for making work such a pleasure; I truly appreciate Jessica Haught, Dave Krech, Melanie Stimeling, and Suzanne Weise.

Our faculty is a collegial group of friends and scholars. Thanks especially to Provost Joyce McConnell, Dean Greg Bowman and the Arthur B. Hodges Summer Research Grant for graciously supporting my work.

Nothing means more to me than my family. John, Gideon, and Hank — thanks for your love and support.

Hollee Schwartz Temple
June 2018

West Virginia Legal Research

Chapter One

The Research Process

I. Introduction to West Virginia Legal Research

Consider this: most new law firm associates spend between 40% and 60% of their work hours conducting legal research.[1] Further, a recent study of law students working at large American firms concluded that summer associates devote between 50% and 100% of their time to legal research.[2] If you want to stand out in a challenging legal marketplace, excel at legal research.

The West Virginia Rules of Professional Conduct further elevate the role of legal research, acknowledging that courts will rely on the legal authorities that lawyers provide. Under the lawyer's duty of candor to the court, lawyers assume an ethical duty to disclose relevant legal authority—even legal authority that is detrimental to a client's position but not raised by opposing counsel.[3] With such an obligation, you can see why quality legal research is so highly valued in the profession.

While the fundamentals of legal research do not vary across American jurisdictions, this text focuses on the resources and analysis needed to conduct comprehensive legal research in West Virginia. When applicable, readers are given information on conducting similar federal legal research. And of course, the text provides instruction in both print and electronic legal research, pro-

---

1. Lexis Nexis, Hiring Partners Reveal New Attorney Readiness For Real World Practice 1 (2015), *available at* https://www.lexisnexis.com/documents/pdf/20150325064926_large.pdf.

2. LexisNexis, Summer Associates Identify Writing and Legal Research Skills Required on the Job 2 (2016), http://www.lexisnexis.com/documents/pdf/20161109032544_large.pdf.

3. W. Va. R. Prof'l Conduct 3.3.

viding at least a glimpse (and often a deeper look) at the most popular and efficient options.

The transition to the electronic research age has changed the face of legal research. A decade ago, research professors could demonstrate a linear process, and researchers could trust that if they followed the meticulous steps from point A to point Z, the process would be complete.

But because of the breadth of information now available online, today's researchers often prefer a different approach. For many, a Google search is a natural starting point — and there is nothing wrong with that. In a sense, where legal researchers used to march through a legal maze to a definitive finish line, today's researchers are dropping in halfway through the labyrinth. But as long as the researcher stops at all of the key turning points on the path, the same results can be achieved — and sometimes much more efficiently. Thus, this text intends to present a research method that will transcend books, the Internet, mobile apps, and even "the next best thing" that comes along.

II. Understanding the Types of Legal Authority

All American law — state and federal — finds its roots in one or more of the three branches of government. A review of the branches and the types of law produced by each is a good starting place.

The legislative branch, whether the West Virginia Legislature or United States Congress, enacts laws reflecting public policy. These laws are called statutes, and eventually land in robust volumes known as legislative codes.

The executive branch, headed by the West Virginia Governor or the President of the United States, is charged with carrying out the laws enacted by the legislative branch. To achieve that mission, the executive branch issues rules and regulations (the terms are used interchangeably) through the government's administrative agencies. These regulations are codified in sets known as the Code of State Rules in West Virginia, and on the federal side, the Code of Federal Regulations.

The judicial branch, whether the West Virginia Supreme Court of Appeals or the Supreme Court of the United States, interprets laws to decide controversies between litigants. Courts may decide cases by applying statutes, by interpreting a constitutional provision, or by using the common law to find similarities or differences in the way courts have previously decided matters. Their opinions eventually appear in case reporters, which are chronological, bound volumes of court cases.

Legal researchers typically divide the law into two spheres: secondary authorities and primary authorities. Secondary authorities can be likened to a researcher's fairy godmother; in essence, someone has done the research for you and collected it in a readable format. For most research topics, a secondary source is the best starting place, as it provides the researcher with both background on the topic and a breadcrumb trail to leading primary sources.

No matter what the legal question, researchers should aim to locate primary mandatory authority—constitutional provisions, statutes, administrative regulations, or judicial opinions—that discuss the legal issue under consideration.

Researchers also draw a distinction between mandatory and persuasive authorities, which carry the weight that you might expect. Courts must follow mandatory (also called "binding") authorities, while persuasive authorities do not need to be followed. They might persuade a judge, but they might not.

The setting of the legal question at issue sometimes determines whether an authority is deemed to be mandatory or persuasive. For example, a West Virginia Supreme Court of Appeals case would be mandatory authority for a circuit court within the state. A circuit court in the neighboring state of Ohio, however, would view the same case as merely persuasive. In other words, Ohio courts could choose to be persuaded by the West Virginia case, but would not be required to follow it.

Finally, keep in mind that some authorities will never rise above their "persuasive" designation. For example, a law review article, newspaper article, or blog post might provide excellent background and context, but because the author was neither a judge, legislature, or agency, the source will always be classified as persuasive.

Table 1-1 shows the branches of West Virginia government and the type of authority issued by each branch. Table 1-2 demonstrates the hierarchy of authority for West Virginia legal research sources.

III. Overview of the Research Process

A. Start Smart: Identify Issues and Understand the Scope of Your Project

It is normal to feel overwhelmed at the beginning of a legal research project—even experienced researchers can struggle. But before you open a single

Table 1-1. West Virginia Legal Authority at a Glance

Government Branch	Type of Authority	Issued By
Legislative	Statutes, Session Laws	West Virginia General Assembly (Senate, House of Delegates)
Judicial	Opinions (Cases)	West Virginia Supreme Court of Appeals
Executive	Administrative Rules and Regulations, Executive Orders, Attorney General Opinions	West Virginia Administrative Agencies, Governor, Attorney General

book or run a single search, you can take a step that will make a big difference. Get the information you need to succeed with your research, or "start smart."

Because many newer attorneys are intimidated by the prospect of a legal research project, they don't ask crucial questions that will help them identify

Table 1-2. Hierarchy of Authority in West Virginia Legal Research

	Mandatory Authority	Persuasive Authority
Primary Authority	• US Constitution and US Supreme Court cases (for federal constitutional issues) • WV Constitution • WV Statutes • WV Administrative Rules • Opinions of WV Supreme Court • WV Rules of Practice, Procedure, and Professional Conduct	• Opinions of other state or federal courts interpreting or applying similar statutory provisions • Opinions of courts in other jurisdictions involving similar common law issues • Non-binding parts of opinions of WV courts (dicta, concurring, and dissenting opinions) • Similar statutes or rules in other jurisdictions
Secondary Authority		• Treatises • Restatements • Law review articles • Legal encyclopedias • Dictionaries

issues and understand the scope of the project. Before you begin the actual legal research process, make sure that you have asked and received answers to the following questions:

- **Are there any materials related to this case that I may review?**
  Often times, a file has been created in paper or electronically, but the supervising attorney does not share this material with the researcher. This is a mistake, as the researcher can develop familiarity with both the facts and key legal concepts from reviewing these documents. Even if you are researching a discrete legal issue, reviewing the file can help you generate search terms and generally understand the issues before you dive into the details. Always ask for the file!

- **What is the expected timeline for this project?**
  While research often takes longer than the supervising attorney expects, it is helpful to understand the general expectations before you get started. This way, if you find that the project is progressing nicely but that you will not complete it in the expected timeframe, you can alert the supervisor and make adjustments accordingly.

- **What is the expected final work product?**
  Not every legal research project will result in a full-blown memorandum of law. Sometimes a supervisor is hoping for a short memo summarizing leading cases; other times she might want a concise email with cases attached. Confirm the final work product expectations before you begin.

- **What jurisdictions should I pursue?**
  Jurisdiction is a threshold question for legal researchers. You must determine which law (e.g., federal, state, and which circuits or states specifically) will apply to the research project before you begin. And you should confirm whether your supervisor wants you to limit your research to a particular jurisdiction. (For example, if West Virginia case law does not produce any mandatory authority on the issue, would your supervisor like you to search in other state courts?)

- **Are there any specialized resources you would recommend?**
  Specialized materials, like those developed for Continuing Legal Education programs (discussed in Chapter 8), often provide practical information that is hard to locate in more traditional legal resources. If you are working on a narrow legal issue (often times, the more local an issue, the narrower), be sure to ask a supervisor or librarian whether there are any recently published materials that address the issue. For

instance, the West Virginia Continuing Legal Education office recently published materials for a seminar relating to the development of shale gas in the state — *Litigation Relating to the Development of the Marcellus Shale.* You can see why these materials would be helpful to a researcher focusing on the shale topic. The authorities covered in seminar materials might not yet be available in more traditional sources, like legal encyclopedias.

- **What else do I need to know?**
  As you are gathering this preliminary information, ask the supervising attorney if there are any questions that you should have asked but didn't. Because it causes the supervisor to stop and think about the totality of the project, it often yields the most valuable information.

B. Consider Your Research Path Possibilities

Once you have answered these important questions, it is time to consider which tools will help you conduct research most efficiently. The best legal researchers typically employ a variety of tools — books, Internet searches, commercial database reviews, to name a few — to ensure that they have thoroughly scoured the universe of legal research possibilities. While this book's goal is to give you the skills you need to conduct effective legal research regardless of the path you choose, newer researchers could benefit from a brief introduction to the most commonly used tools.

Up until a few years ago, research professors cautioned students against broad Internet searches, as the results were unpredictable and often led novice researchers astray. Students who didn't understand the weight of legal authorities made the mistakes of citing blog posts as authority and quoting incorrect passages that hadn't been verified.

However, with search engine improvements and instruction on how to assess the validity of Internet-based sources (see Chapter 9), legal researchers have begun to realize the benefits of free online searching. A Google search might even be a good starting place, as it can help you find background information quickly and might uncover citations to possible cases. But you can't simply review the top three results and stop there — legal research requires much more.

Fortunately for today's legal researchers, the newest versions of the favored commercial research systems WestlawNext and Lexis Advance now offer Google-like searching options. These new interfaces offer a familiar search bar across the top. Researchers simply filter their jurisdictional choices through a tab that sits next to the search bar, and artificial intelligence produces reasonably good results. Bloomberg Law, a relative newcomer to the legal research market, offers a similarly intuitive interface, and also integrates the company's renowned news, company, and financial data. Bloomberg has recently broadened its offerings to include access to secondary materials published by the Bureau of National Affairs (BNA), as well as a simplified interface for finding federal court dockets on Public Access to Court Electronic Records, commonly known as PACER.

Some of the less expensive subscription services, such as the Fastcase system provided free to all members of the West Virginia State Bar Association, require a bit more finesse. Because the algorithms are not as advanced as WestlawNext and Lexis Advance, systems like Fastcase typically produce better results through selection of the appropriate database and then a terms-and-connectors search (also known as Boolean searching). This method allows you to enter key terms and then specify the relationship between those terms. For example, you might ask the system to produce cases from West Virginia that discuss the terms workplace and safety. "And" is the connector that will tell the search engine to look for both of these words. You can further specify that you want to see them in the same paragraph or sentence. Filtering tools can help researchers find more focused results.

That being said, Fastcase has come a long way. Though it has fewer bells and whistles than its more expensive competitors, many practitioners can find almost everything they need through Fastcase's nationwide research system. For example, Fastcase offers West Virginia cases beginning in 1864, and also includes most U.S. Supreme Court cases, federal circuit court cases, federal district court cases, federal bankruptcy court cases, and most state cases back to 1950. Further, the new "type-ahead" search in Fastcase is a powerful feature that predictively autocompletes queries by suggesting the most likely search phrases. Fastcase ranks these suggested terms using a ranking algorithm, much like WestlawNext and Lexis Advance.

Further, if you are looking for primary authority such as statutes or cases, you may be able find reasonably accurate results via free websites. (Chapter 9 discusses these possibilities in detail.) Books, and particularly professional materials (discussed in Chapter 8), may round out your research trail. Regardless of which paths you choose, it is essential that you consider the universe of possible authorities and ensure that you have located the most relevant results. A suggested process for meeting these goals is discussed in the remainder of this section.

C. Generate a List of Search Terms

Once you feel confident about your assignment and have considered the routes you might travel to reach your research goals, it's time for some preliminary searching. The goal is to uncover search terms that will focus your research. You might conduct a broad Internet search to learn more about the terms that frequently arise in discussions of your topic, or they may automatically pop up as you begin your initial searching in the commercial databases. A book or an article also could help you generate the search terms you need to later execute an efficient online search.

D. Create an Authority Chart

Effective researchers develop tools to ensure that they have reviewed all eligible sources. They also find a systematic way for recording their research results. An authority chart or checklist works well for completing these tasks. Some researchers prefer to create electronic charts and then to link to the authorities as they record their results.

Table 1-3 shows a blank authority chart that would work well for a West Virginia state law research problem. Of course, the chart could be adapted for any other state, or for a federal research problem.

Table 1-3. Blank Research Authority Chart

Primary Mandatory Authority	Secondary Authority
• Statute(s) • Case(s) • Regulations	• Legal Encyclopedia • Law Review/Other Periodical
Primary Persuasive Authority	**Possible Search Terms?**

E. Start by Consulting Secondary Sources That Will Lead You to Primary Authorities

Begin on the right side of the chart with secondary sources, checking to see which general interest articles discuss the topic at issue. As you perform searches in each major resource, record possible authorities to review after you've completed your initial secondary source research. Also, as you come across new key terms, add them to the "possible search terms" box in the bottom right-hand corner.

Next, pull the secondary sources you have noted on your chart, and skim them. This will help you to determine which sources thoroughly discuss your legal issue. Focus on your favorite few and read them in more depth. As you read these authorities, you will find leads to primary citations, which you should then record under the primary authorities category on your chart. At this point, you could also conduct an online search by using the terms you recorded in the bottom right quadrant. Again, list any good possibilities in the appropriate block of the chart.

F. Use Your Authority Chart — Retrieve, Read, and Evaluate Primary Authority

Once you have populated the primary side of your authority chart, read these authorities and determine which discuss your issue most completely. Cross off the sources that don't fit the bill and highlight the authorities you like best. (Note: Some of the categories will not always apply. For example, you will probably not find any relevant statutes or regulations for a West Virginia common law issue. Once you have determined that those categories are inapplicable, delete them from the chart.)

Table 1-4 shows an in-progress authority chart. Of course, you can adopt this template to suit your needs and personal preferences. Just be sure to indicate which sources have been checked and which remain. This will prove very valuable if you return to the project after a period of time and cannot remember exactly which sources you previously consulted.

G. Confirm Validity and Currency of Sources

After you have selected the sources that best answer the legal question you have been asked to research, you need to make sure the sources are still good

Table 1-4. In-Progress Authority Chart

Primary Mandatory Authority	Secondary Authority
Statute(s) W. Va. Code Ann. §61-2-1 (West 2017) W. Va. Code Ann. §61-2-4 (West 2017) **Case(s)** *State v. McMillion*, 138 S.E. 732 (W. Va. 1927) *State v. Harden*, 679 S.E.2d 628 (W. Va. 2009) *State v. Steele*, 359 S.E.2d 558 (W. Va. 1987) *State v. McGuire*, 490 S.E.2d 912, 924 (W. Va. 1997) **Regulations** None found	**Legal Encyclopedia** Jimmie E. Tinsley, *Criminal Law: The Battered Woman Defense*, 34 Am. Jur. Proof of Facts 2d (1983) **Law Review/Other Periodical** Devin C. Daines, *State v. Harden: Muddying the Waters of Self-Defense Law in West Virginia*, 113 W. Va. L. Rev. 971 (2011) Find others?
Primary Persuasive Authority	**Possible Search Terms**
Not needed	Abuse, domestic abuse, battered woman, self-defense

law. Citator services like Shepard's and KeyCite (explained in depth in Chapter 5) will help you accomplish this task efficiently.

H. When to Stop

Newer researchers often feel nervous about completing a research project; they fear that they have missed the golden chalice that contains all of the answers.

But typically, whether a research project is complete should not be a guessing game. Just ask yourself the following questions. First, have you consulted all of the categories on the checklist and thoroughly checked for authorities in each area? Next, have you noticed that the same primary authorities keep popping up repeatedly—for example, does a single case appear in a law review article, encyclopedia, and annotations to the state code? When that happens, you know that you have found a leading authority. You will not be able to discuss every case you uncover in your work product, so once you have found a collection of relevant authorities, it is time to stop searching for authorities and begin organizing your analysis.

If, however, you do not find yourself coming upon the same citations repeatedly, you may need to return to earlier steps in the process.

I. Convert Your Findings to a Concise Written Product

After you have completed your research, your supervisor will likely ask for some sort of written report, which could take many forms. You might be asked to synthesize the legal rules that apply to your project and provide case examples. (This is where you combine your most important findings and offer some illustrations of the rule in action.) You might be asked to collect the key cases and provide summaries. Or you might be asked to thoroughly analyze the client's matter via a full-blown legal memorandum.

No matter what the assignment, and even if you are not responsible for writing the final legal document, recognize that someone will rely on the accuracy of your research in preparing documents that will probably be submitted to clients and courts. To that end, be sure that the rules you present are accurate, complete, concise, and valid.

IV. Organization of This Book

This book aims to give readers the tools they need to conduct effective and efficient legal research in West Virginia. In certain instances, the book also provides guidance on replicating the research process for federal issues. (For example, Chapter 6 on Researching State Administrative Law discusses not only how to research state agency rules in West Virginia but also how to conduct similar research at the federal level.)

Throughout this book, you will find discussions of both print and electronic methods of locating legal materials. You also will find advice on citing and updating your findings. Finally, at the end of most chapters, you will find an alphabetical list of "Additional Resources" that guides you to the most relevant Internet links.

Chapter 1 has introduced you to the process of legal research, and the remaining chapters teach you how to conduct West Virginia legal research in a variety of ways. Because the research process often begins in secondary sources, Chapter 2 teaches you how to locate and use secondary materials.

Chapters 3 and 4 turn to primary authority. Chapter 3 discusses the highest of all primary authorities in West Virginia, the state Constitution. In Chapter

4, you will learn about the legislative process and the creation of West Virginia statutes.

Chapter 5 addresses case law and the many ways to find it. Chapter 6 discusses administrative law, a popular arena for many West Virginia practitioners.

In Chapters 7 and 8, researchers learn about some of the intricacies of West Virginia practice. Chapter 7 addresses ethics and specialized court rules for the state. Chapter 8 introduces West Virginia-focused professional materials that can provide practical resources for legal researchers.

Chapter 9 acknowledges the growing trend of Internet-based legal research. It suggests a process for conducting online research and nominates top sites. While this book refers most frequently to Lexis and Westlaw products—long the industry standards for electronic legal research—Chapter 9 discusses many other online (and often free) alternatives. Chapter 10 rounds out the book with a discussion of legal citation, with a focus on West Virginia sources.

V. A Word about Citation

Throughout this book, you will see repeated references to "citation" or "cites." Documents written for legal audiences must conform to specific rules of citation; West Virginia lawyers typically consult the *Bluebook* as a citation guide. However, local rules sometimes dictate that lawyers follow a different format than that prescribed by the *Bluebook*. Chapter 10 covers citation rules for West Virginia (and beyond) in depth.

Chapter Two

Researching Secondary Sources

I. Introduction to Secondary Sources

A. Secondary Sources as a Road Map

If you have ever been lost along one of West Virginia's legendary country roads, you know the value of a navigational tool.

Just as it makes sense to scan a map or set of directions before taking off on a trip, your initial time in the legal research journey may be best invested by reviewing secondary sources. Through them, you will not only become familiar with the legal landscape, but you will also discover the landmark cases and other important primary authorities.

There are many types of secondary sources: legal encyclopedias, treatises on specific legal subjects, law reviews, and bar journal articles, just to name a few. While practice and professional materials are also of great value to West Virginia lawyers (Chapter 8 discusses these resources in depth), this chapter focuses on the more basic secondary source materials.

B. Choosing a Secondary Source: Learn About Your Tools

The legal researcher typically does best with the most narrow, specific secondary source available. For example, a national legal encyclopedia like *American Jurisprudence* or *Corpus Juris Secundum* might produce a lead to a key West Virginia case, but you are much more likely to find the answer quickly in *Michie's Jurisprudence*, an encyclopedia of West Virginia and Virginia law.

It takes time to learn which secondary sources best suit your needs. If you are researching an area of law that is completely unfamiliar, an encyclopedia or treatise might be the best starting place. After learning the basics of a legal topic, you then might explore the details with a law review article.

For less experienced researchers, the best course of action is almost always to ask someone with more experience for suggestions. When in doubt, ask a librarian!

C. Updating and Citing Secondary Sources

While some secondary sources receive regular updates, some are sent to the publisher and never updated again. For example, legal encyclopedias often include annual pocket parts—supplemental pages inserted in the back of a volume. (Or, encyclopedia updates may be published even more frequently in online versions.) Law review articles, however, are published at a moment in time and, while new periodicals may comment on their material, a new "version" of a previously published law review article will not appear. Again, consult a librarian to feel confident that you are using secondary sources that are current.

Lawyers typically do not cite to secondary sources in briefs and memos. Instead, they scour these materials to efficiently find leads to the most important primary authorities. Law students, on the other hand, may have more occasions to cite to secondary sources, particularly when writing academic papers and law review notes.

II. Secondary Sources and the Legal Researcher

A. Legal Encyclopedias

1. Using Legal Encyclopedias

Legal encyclopedias are perhaps the most valuable legal resources available, particularly for newer researchers.

National and state legal encyclopedias serve three key functions: providing background on unfamiliar areas of law, identifying related legal issues, and offering citations to relevant primary and secondary sources. In a sense, a more experienced researcher has taken the guesswork out of a new subject, providing readable background information and cites to the key authorities that a supervisor would expect in a discussion of the topic. As such, encyclopedias save time; someone has done the heavy lifting for you!

Unless your supervisor has provided a specific citation, you would typically start working in an encyclopedia by identifying a topic in the index. The index will lead you to articles on a variety of subjects within the encyclopedia's volumes.

a. Michie's Jurisprudence: *State Legal Encyclopedia for West Virginia*

Long a cornerstone reference guide for West Virginia and Virginia practitioners, *Michie's Jurisprudence* offers encyclopedic treatment of the civil and criminal law of both states. This encyclopedia provides background on most legal topics, exposing novice researchers to the key concepts while analyzing case law, statutes, rules, and regulations. In addition to the wealth of primary authorities cited, this encyclopedia also offers extensive references to other secondary sources. With such a wealth of knowledge in one source, it is not surprising that many West Virginia practitioners begin their searches in *Michie's Jurisprudence*. Figure 2-1 illustrates a typical page from *Michie's Jurisprudence*.

b. National Encyclopedias

For most West Virginia researchers, the leading national encyclopedias, *American Jurisprudence* (Am. Jur.) and *Corpus Juris Secundum* (C.J.S.), may contain too much information on a subject. Because these national encyclopedias explain the law in a large number of states, the entries are very long — and often times omit citations to West Virginia authority.

c. American Law Reports

Though not technically a legal encyclopedia, *American Law Reports* (A.L.R.) is often used in a similar way by legal researchers. A.L.R. is a hybrid secondary source — part case reporter, as it contains opinions, but also part background source, with articles that describe how the legal issues in that novel case have been treated in the statutes and case law of other jurisdictions. The A.L.R. is more like an encyclopedia than like a law journal in its discussion of legal issues; the articles are typically not critical and instead lay out the national legal landscape for an area of law. For researchers tackling questions of first impression, the A.L.R. provides a quick source for determining how other jurisdictions have handled these issues. For example, you can use the A.L.R. to determine whether a West Virginia case represents the majority or minority rule in other United States jurisdictions.

Researchers find articles, also known as annotations, in the A.L.R. through a topical index system similar to those used for searching encyclopedias. If your topic of interest happens to be covered in an A.L.R. annotation, you will save hours of research time, as the author has, in a sense, performed the research and compiled the results on your behalf.

Figure 2-1. Screenshot of *Michie's Jurisprudence*

III. CONSTRUCTION AND INTERPRETATION OF CONSTITUTIONS.

§ 7. Generally. — Questions of constitutional construction are in the main governed by the same general rules as those applied in statutory construction.[19] The courts approach constitutional questions with great caution, and regard the interpretation and application of constitutional provisions as among the most important as well as delicate and difficult duties which they have to perform. They must endeavor to hold up the hands of the law-making body, but, to do so effectively and in such a way as to command public respect and confidence, they must not, for mere reasons of convenience or expediency, hesitate to condemn an act which plainly violates the fundamental law.[20]

Where the constitution is clear in its terms and of plain interpretation to any ordinary and reasonable mind, there is no room for construction, and it would be mischievous and unlawful to assume it.[1] If the intention is manifest from

18. State ex rel. Boards of Educ. v. Chafin, 376 S.E.2d 113 (W. Va. 1988).

19. State ex rel. Brotherton v. Blankenship, 157 W. Va. 100, 207 S.E.2d 421 (1973).

Questions of constitutional construction are in the main governed by the same general rules applied in statutory construction. Winkler v. State, Sch. Bldg. Auth., 434 S.E.2d 420 (W. Va. 1993); State ex rel. Robb v. Caperton, 191 W. Va. 492, 446 S.E.2d 714 (1994); State ex rel. Holmes v. Gainer, 191 W. Va. 686, 447 S.E.2d 887 (1994).

20. Martin v. Com., 126 Va. 603, 102 S.E. 77 (1920).

As to interpretation and construction, see the title Interpretation and Construction.

For an article, "Constitutional Developments in Five War Years," see 32 Va. L. Rev. 461. For an article, "The Doctrinal Development of the Tenth Amendment," see 51 W. Va. L.Q. 227. For a digest of cases decided in the 1965 term of the Supreme Court of the United States and touching constitutional issues, see 8 Wm. & Mary L. Rev. 49 (1966). For a note, "Prospectivity and Retroactivity of Supreme Court Constitutional Interpretations," see 5 U. Rich. L. Rev. 129 (1970).

1. May v. Topping, 65 W. Va. 656, 64 S.E. 848 (1909). See State v. Conley, 118 W. Va. 508, 190 S.E. 908 (1937); Roanoke v. Michael's Bakery Corp., 180 Va. 132, 21 S.E.2d 788 (1942); Flesher v. Board of Review, 138 W. Va. 765, 77 S.E.2d 890 (1953); State v. West, 145 W. Va. 498, 116 S.E.2d 398 (1960), quoting M.J.; State ex rel. Smith v. Gore, 150 W. Va. 71, 143 S.E.2d 791 (1965), commented on in 68 W. Va. L. R---

106 S.E.2d 636 (1959); Appalachian Power Co. v. County Court of Mercer County, 146 W. Va. 118, 118 S.E.2d 531 (1961), commented on in 63 W. Va. L. Rev. 357 (1961); Robertson v. Hatcher, 148 W. Va. 239, 135 S.E.2d 675 (1964); State ex rel. City of Princeton v. Buckner, 377 S.E.2d 139 (W. Va. 1988).

Constitutional language clear in its meaning need not and should not be construed but should be accorded its ordinary connotation and applied. Foster v. Cooper, 155 W. Va. 619, 186 S.E.2d 837 (1972); State ex rel. Casey v. Pauley, 210 S.E.2d 649 (1974); State ex rel. Maloney v. McCartney, 159 W. Va. 513, 223 S.E.2d 607 (1976); State ex rel. Dunbar v. Stone, 159 W. Va. 331, 221 S.E.2d 791 (1976); State ex rel. Rushford v. Meador, 165 W. Va. 48, 267 S.E.2d 169 (1980).

Courts are not concerned with the wisdom or expediencies of constitutional provisions, and the duty of the judiciary is merely to carry out the provisions of the plain language stated in the constitution. State ex rel. Casey v. Pauley, 158 W. Va. 298, 210 S.E.2d 649 (1974).

The West Virginia Supreme Court of Appeals is empowered to construe, interpret and apply provisions of the constitution but may not add to, distort or ignore the plain mandate thereof. State ex rel. Bagley v. Blankenship, 161 W. Va. 630, 246 S.E.2d 99 (1978).

Where a provision of a constitution is clear in its terms and of plain interpretation to any ordinary and reasonable mind, it should be applied and not construed. Jarrett Printing Co. v. Riley, 188 W. Va. 393, 424 S.E.2d 738 (1992);

Source: Reprinted with permission of LexisNexis.

2. Citing Encyclopedias as a Source of Authority

It is rare for legal researchers to cite to encyclopedias; instead, use them to find leads to the best primary sources.

B. Treatises

1. Overview

A legal treatise is a scholarly legal publication summarizing the law in a particular area, such as copyright law or tax planning. The term "legal treatise" is a broad one, used to describe books written for practicing lawyers, legal textbooks, and even explanatory texts that non-lawyers might peruse.

Legal researchers categorize treatises as secondary authorities. They are typically used to review and update knowledge in an area of law, and as a starting place for locating the key primary authorities. In law school, professors sometimes assign portions of treatises to cover legal subjects at a more detailed level than casebooks provide. Further, American law students often use special treatises called hornbooks to supplement their casebooks. These hornbooks typically contain a condensed version of the materials written by recognized legal scholars in multi-volume treatises.

2. Finding and Using Treatises

With a collection of more than 300,000 volumes, the George R. Farmer, Jr. Law Library at West Virginia University College of Law is the largest law library in West Virginia. The library maintains a core collection of federal and regional reporters, federal and state codes, administrative law materials, and many secondary sources, including treatises. Tables 2-1 and 2-2 list major treatises specific to West Virginia as well as general treatises commonly used by West Virginia lawyers. (Of course, practice specialties will dictate which treatises will prove to be the most useful. For instance, lawyers practicing in the social security area may cling to Thomas Bush's *Social Security Disability Practice*, while an oil and gas attorney might never have an occasion to open it.) Many of the treatises in Tables 2-1 and 2-2 can be found through commercial databases. Refer to Chapter 9 for more information on conducting online searches.

You can discover which legal treatises are available in the West Virginia University (WVU) collection through MountainLynx, the university's library catalog system. WVU students and public patrons with library cards can borrow books from the WVU Law Library. WVU law students also can request treatises and related books from other WVU Libraries (such as the WVU Downtown

Table 2-1. Key West Virginia Treatises

Handbook on Evidence for West Virginia Lawyers

Handbook on West Virginia Criminal Procedure

Litigation Handbook on West Virginia Rules of Civil Procedure

Michie's Jurisprudence of Virginia and West Virginia

Trial Handbook for West Virginia Lawyers

West Virginia Judicial Benchbook for Child Abuse and Neglect Proceedings

West Virginia State Bar Practice Handbook

Table 2-2. Treatises Commonly Used by West Virginia Lawyers

Farnsworth on Contracts

Federal Practice and Procedure, Wright & Miller

Moore's Federal Practice

Nimmer on Copyright

The New Wigmore: A Treatise on Evidence

Campus Library or Health Sciences Library), and these items will be delivered to the WVU Law Library Circulation Desk. If the item you are looking for is not available through the WVU Libraries, the E-ZBorrow system allows students to search within the Pennsylvania Academic Library Consortium. As a final option, WorldCat provides worldwide searching. WVU reference librarians can assist legal researchers with these options.

C. Legal Periodicals

1. Overview

Law reviews (also known as law journals) typically fill the most shelves in the secondary source section of any law library. There are literally hundreds of journals, with all accredited law schools publishing at least one primary journal and some publishing multiple specialty journals.

Law reviews contain articles written by law professors, legal experts, attorneys, and even some law students. In legal periodicals, academics analyze, describe, and comment on the law. Law reviews are typically affiliated with law schools, but there are a few non-academic publishers. Those familiar with the peer review process in other academic disciplines may be surprised to learn that students typically select and edit the law review articles published by law schools.

West Virginia University College of Law publishes the state's primary law review, the *West Virginia Law Review*. It is the nation's fourth oldest and publishes three issues each year on a wide range of legal topics. Like many law reviews, the *West Virginia Law Review* now publishes both in print and electronically.

Some law reviews focus on a specific legal topic. For instance, the *Energy Law Journal* (published through a partnership between the Energy Bar Association and the University of Tulsa College of Law) is of interest to energy law practitioners within the state, even though it only periodically addresses West Virginia's laws and regulations specifically. Similarly, the *Texas Wesleyan Law Review* conducts an annual Survey on Oil & Gas that includes items from each state, including West Virginia.

Legal periodicals provide excellent introductions to obscure or cutting-edge areas of law, and for researchers who are not familiar with a subject, they provide useful background. In newly developing areas of law, law review articles often cover topics that have not been addressed by more general encyclopedias, treatises, or practice manuals. Legal researchers often use law review articles to find leads to the leading primary sources on a legal topic; these articles also can be used to master the leading arguments for law reform.

In addition to law reviews, legal researchers can turn to legal periodicals known as bar journals and legal newspapers for coverage of recent news and items of general interest to the legal community. *The West Virginia Lawyer* is the official magazine of the West Virginia State Bar. This magazine is distributed to all members of the West Virginia State Bar on a quarterly basis. Approximately three weeks after the print edition is distributed, an electronic version is made available on the State Bar website. Click the "News & Events" tab to see PDF versions of the magazine. In addition, members of the State Bar receive a weekly "Bar Blast" e-newsletter that chronicles upcoming events and items of interest for West Virginia lawyers.

While legal researchers may casually refer to any information printed in a legal periodical as an article, the contents of legal periodicals vary in weight and authoritative value. For example, an article written by a judge or professor would have more weight than a note or comment written by a law student. The table of contents at the beginning of the periodical issue typically identifies the author's credentials.

2. Finding and Using Legal Periodicals

Commercial databases like Lexis, Westlaw, and Bloomberg Law provide the easiest way to locate legal periodicals; you can search for and obtain your findings in an integrated search. Traditional indexes of legal periodicals provide listings of articles by topic and author, but then you must find the articles in an additional research step. This may be why print versions of the two major indexes for legal periodicals, the *Index to Legal Periodicals & Books* and *Current Law Index*, are becoming increasingly rare. The WVU College of Law does provide patrons with both hard copy and electronic access to these resources.

Further, several specialty databases are geared toward researchers looking for legal periodicals. For example, LegalTrac is an expanded, web-based version of the print *Current Law Index*, but it only includes selected full-text articles. Similarly, the *Current Index to Legal Periodicals*, published by the Gallagher Law Library at the University of Washington, may prove to be a useful tool for locating journal articles; the WVU College of Law maintains print and electronic subscriptions to this service.

Many law firms and law libraries now provide access to HeinOnline, a service designed to help legal researchers find law review articles. HeinOnline offers an image-based searchable database, so researchers can both find relevant law review articles and see them just as they first appeared. (This can be particularly helpful for articles featuring graphs and tables.) HeinOnline provides comprehensive coverage dating back to the inaugural issues of more than 1,500 law and law-related periodicals.

While HeinOnline is a valuable tool for finding specific law review articles when the citation is known, it is not the easiest tool for searching by topic. Nevertheless, HeinOnline does provide an index system that organizes law review articles by topic, just as a book index or the subject headings of a library catalog would. They are well suited for browsing in a general area, but sometimes cumbersome for finding a narrowly focused article. In contrast, commercial databases allow researchers to look for words in either an "abstract" or the full text of a journal article, so you typically get results more quickly.

Finally, don't forget that citators such as Shepard's and KeyCite also may generate results that lead researchers to on-point legal periodicals. Citators are discussed in detail in Chapter 5.

In addition, law professors and other scholars use the Social Science Research Network (SSRN) to share published articles and works in progress. SSRN offers free searching and downloading.

Finally, Google Scholar provides a free academic search engine for law review articles. Google Scholar searches often redirect researchers to articles in the HeinOnline database.

WVU law students can log into most legal databases from any location with off-campus access codes. Simply ask a librarian for a password or check the complete list of electronic authorization codes for WVU law students through the Law Library's TWEN page.

3. Citing Law Review Articles as Authority

Law students rely heavily on law review articles when writing academic papers. Practitioners, on the other hand, cite to law review articles sparingly, preferring primary authorities. That being said, law review articles written by particularly influential judges and professors are sometimes cited in briefs to the court.

D. Dictionaries

Legal researchers, and law students in particular, often consult legal dictionaries to understand the meaning of unfamiliar words. *Black's Law Dictionary* is the industry standard, and it is now available as a mobile phone application.

Like many secondary sources, dictionaries serve primarily as a learning tool and are not typically cited in memoranda or briefs unless there is no other definition available. Legal researchers can find most legal definitions (including earlier editions of *Black's Law Dictionary*) via free websites or with their Westlaw passwords.

Researchers often overlook West's *Words and Phrases*—a volume of the digests that functions like a dictionary and allows researchers to find state-specific definitions of certain terms. You would not cite to *Words and Phrases*, but the cases included there may prove to offer useful definitions.

E. Restatements (Annotated)

The American Law Institute, an organization of legal academics and practitioners, publishes *Restatements of the Law*, a set of legal treatises on the general principles of common law, broken down by subject matter. Restatements condense the common law into a set of principles or rules. Restatements explain what the law is or, in some cases, what the authors think it ought to be. While the Restatements are not binding, courts can adopt them as persuasive authority. When this happens at a higher court level, the provisions become binding in a sense, as lower courts must then follow suit.

Each Restatement section includes a Black Letter principle, Comments and Illustrations, and a detailed case discussion. Courts often pay close attention to Restatement sections, as they restate the already-established law and, on issues of first impression, demonstrate the current trend. Law students often come across the *Restatement of Torts* and *Restatement of Contracts* in the first-year curriculum.

III. Citing Secondary Sources

Details on citation form for secondary sources appear in Chapter 10, but for quick reference, here are some examples:

- West Virginia: 20 M.J. *Wills* § 42 (2012)
  Evan Olds, Note, *Give It to Me Uniformly: West Virginia Wants Initial Disclosure*, 115 W. Va. L. Rev. 363 (2012)

- Federal: 79 Am. Jur. 2d *Wills* § 405 (2012)
  6 C.J.S. *Appearances* § 6 (2012)

IV. Additional Resources

Note: Some West Virginia-specific secondary sources are explored at more length in Chapter 8, as they are more likely to be used in connection with practice-oriented (as opposed to academic) research.

Current Index to Legal Periodicals
    https://lib.law.washington.edu/cilp/cilp.html

Eastern Mineral Law Foundation, white papers and conference materials
    http://emlf.org

E-Z Borrow Service[1]
    http://libraries.wvu.edu/services/borrowing/ezborrow

Foundation of the Energy Law Journal (contains links to Journal online)
    http://www.eba-net.org

George R. Farmer, Jr. Law Library
    http://law.wvu.edu/library

---

1. This service is only available to current West Virginia University students, staff, and faculty.

Google Scholar
    http://scholar.google.com

HeinOnline
    http://home.heinonline.org

Legal Trac Information[2]
    www.gale.cengage.com

Library of Congress Guide to West Virginia Law
    http://www.loc.gov/law/help/guide/states/us-wv.php

Social Science Research Network
    http://www.ssrn.com

Texas Wesleyan Law Review
    http://www.texaswesleyanlawreview.org

West Virginia Law Review
    http://wvlawreview.wvu.edu

The West Virginia Lawyer
    http://www.wvbar.org/news_events_publications/default.aspx

West Virginia State Bar
    http://www.wvbar.org

West Virginia State Bar Practice Handbook
    http://www.wvyounglawyers.com/handbook.html

West Virginia University Libraries
    http://libraries.wvu.edu

WorldCat Library Catalog
    http://www.worldcat.org

---

2. You can access LegalTrac by using the search bar or by selecting "InfoTrac Periodical Solutions," followed by "All Products," followed by "LegalTrac."

Chapter Three

Researching Constitutional Law

"Since through Divine Providence we enjoy the blessings of civil, political and religious liberty, we, the people of West Virginia, in and through the provisions of this Constitution, reaffirm our faith in and constant reliance upon God and seek diligently to promote, preserve and perpetuate good government in the state of West Virginia for the common welfare, freedom and security of ourselves and our posterity."[1]

I. Introduction to Constitutional Law

Legal researchers typically consult constitutions when they need to assess the propriety of governmental actions or the scope of a governing body's authority. Like all Americans, West Virginians are subject to two constitutions: the United States Constitution and a state constitution. Both may prove valuable to legal researchers, as constitutions not only explain the structure of government, but also delineate the relationships between the government, its branches, and the citizenry.

While some lawyers rarely encounter constitutional law issues, others deal with them daily. Clearly, lawyers who deal with election issues and criminal law work with constitutions often. But constitutional issues also creep into areas that you may not typically associate with constitutional law. For example, family law practitioners may research constitutional law when arguing that a parent didn't receive due process in a termination proceeding. Similarly, environmental lawyers may rely upon constitutions when property rights are implicated. Stay alert for constitutional law issues whenever government action comes into play. Many research topics in constitutional law focus on the interpretation of a constitutional provision or amendment, or whether a particular state law passes constitutional muster.

---

1. W. Va. Const. pmbl.

The United States Supreme Court has explicitly acknowledged the rights of state courts to read their constitutions broadly—the civil rights enumerated in state constitutions can provide greater protections than those given by the federal Constitution. Under the Tenth Amendment to the United States Constitution, powers that have not been delegated to the federal government are reserved for state control.[2] Of course, the state of West Virginia cannot provide its citizens with fewer protections or fewer rights than those accorded by the United States Constitution.

II. The History of the West Virginia Constitution

In reflecting upon the West Virginia Constitution, the late West Virginia Supreme Court Justice Franklin D. Cleckley wrote, "As a member of the West Virginia Supreme Court of Appeals, I have learned to revere the West Virginia Constitution. The power that permits me to perform my service for the citizens of this state emanates solely from that document. Indeed, all powers of the Legislative, Executive, and Judicial branches of our state government have been created by it, and the limitations on our powers are also found within it."[3] The West Virginia Constitution enumerates the fundamental principles of the state's governance.

West Virginia has been home to two constitutions; the first was ratified in 1863 and the second in 1872.[4] West Virginia's first constitutional convention, which began in 1861, occurred during a period of widespread conflict over the election of Abraham Lincoln. The convention was a direct response to Virginia's decision to secede from the Union and join the Confederacy.[5] Although the convention's delegates generally agreed that West Virginia's Constitution should model the Virginia Constitution, drafters implemented some significant changes to eliminate perceived injustices that concerned Western Virginians.[6] Some of these changes included equal apportionment based on population, the removal of property qualifications required for voting, equal property tax-

---

2. U.S. Const. amend. X.

3. Franklin D. Cleckley, *Foreword* to Robert M. Bastress, *The West Virginia State Constitution: A Reference Guide*, xix, xix (1995).

4. Robert M. Bastress, *The Constitution of West Virginia*, Oct. 25, 2012, The West Virginia Encyclopedia, http://www.wvencyclopedia.org/articles/1558.

5. *See* Bastress, *supra* note 3, at 9–11.

6. *Id.* at 11.

ation, requirements for the formation of public schools, and a preclusion for governmental borrowing of money.[7] Voters approved the draft of the Constitution and West Virginia's petition for statehood was approved in 1863, making West Virginia the 35th state.[8] Although the government of Virginia consented to West Virginia's statehood, the issue was controversial and had to be settled by the U.S. Supreme Court in 1871.[9] The U.S. Supreme Court held that the constitutionality of West Virginia's statehood was a "political question" that had been settled by Congress.[10]

After the Civil War ended in 1865, the West Virginia Legislature imposed several "disabilities on former Confederates" that made it difficult for former Confederates to vote, use the court system, or hold political office.[11] Not surprisingly, the former Confederates were not happy with these restrictions, and eventually, voters convened a second constitutional convention,[12] which was held in 1872. The new Constitution reformed a few of the legislative enactments that caused hardships to former Confederates.[13]

III. Highlights of the West Virginia Constitution

The West Virginia Constitution contains a preamble, fourteen articles, and seventeen amendments. Table 3-1 lists the Articles of the West Virginia Constitution.

Articles I and II discuss West Virginia's relationship with the United States government and provide a general description of the state. Article III contains West Virginia's Bill of Rights and describes the basic freedoms protected under state law. Article IV explains the state election process.

Articles V through VIII outline the division of power between the Legislative, Executive, and Judicial branches of government and describe their powers. Specifically, Article V calls for a separation of the powers of the three branches. Article VI creates the West Virginia Legislature, composed of a Senate and House of Delegates. Article VII lists the major constitutional executives, which

---

7. Bastress, *supra* note 4.
8. *Id.*
9. Bastress, *supra* note 3, at 13.
10. *Id.* (discussing *State of Virginia v. State of West Virginia*, 78 U.S. 39 (1870)).
11. *Id.* at 16.
12. *Id.* at 18.
13. *Id.* at 18–21.

Table 3-1. Articles of the West Virginia Constitution

Article I	Relations to the Government of the United States
Article II	The State
Article III	Bill of Rights
Article IV	Election and Officers
Article V	Division of Powers
Article VI	The Legislature
Article VII	Executive Department
Article VIII	Judicial Power
Article IX	County Organization
Article X	Taxation and Finance
Article XI	Corporations
Article XII	Education
Article XIII	Land Titles
Article XIV	Amendments

are elected by the people and serve four-year terms. Article VIII creates a state judiciary composed of a supreme court of appeals and circuit courts. While there is currently no intermediate appellate court operating in the state, it is specifically allowed for under this article.

Article IX describes governmental organization at the local level and creates the county offices of county commissioner, prosecuting attorney, sheriff, county clerk, assessor, and surveyor. Article X outlines the state's taxation powers and imposes an equal and uniform requirement for taxation, subject to a few exceptions. Article XI assigns the Legislature power to provide for the organization of all corporations and describes the basic liability of corporations and rights of stockholders.

Article XII ensures the fundamental right to attend a public school without having to pay for an education and creates a state board of education and a state superintendent of schools. Article XIII, which governs land titles, has now been largely repealed; however, it protects land titles obtained from Virginia before West Virginia became a state.

Article XIV creates two ways to amend the West Virginia Constitution: (1) through a constitutional convention or (2) by passage of a two-thirds vote by both houses of the Legislature along with a subsequent passage by the people.

Seventeen amendments follow the articles of the West Virginia Constitution; they address a variety of topics, including veteran bonuses, school funding and maintenance, and road development and maintenance.

IV. Seminal West Virginia Constitutional Law Cases

While it is difficult to designate the most influential constitutional law cases in West Virginia history, the following have significantly influenced West Virginia jurisprudence and may crop up frequently for lawyers undertaking state constitutional law research:

- *Pauley v. Kelly*, 255 S.E.2d 859 (W. Va. 1979): This case brought about major reforms in both the financing and administration of public schools in the state. The Supreme Court of Appeals of West Virginia held that "a thorough and efficient system of free schools"[14] found in Article XII, Section 1 of the West Virginia Constitution made education a fundamental, constitutional right. Furthermore, the Court held that any discriminatory classification in the state's educational financing system couldn't stand under the Equal Protection Clause unless the state could demonstrate a compelling interest.

- *State ex rel. Roy Allen S. v. Stone*, 474 S.E.2d 554 (W. Va. 1996), and *Women's Health Center v. Panepinto*, 446 S.E. 2d 658 (W. Va. 1993): These cases established a substantive due process analysis for fundamental rights and showed the Court's willingness to push the protection of rights beyond what the federal constitution had been construed to provide.

- *State ex rel. West Virginia Citizens Action Group v. West Virginia Economic Development Committee*, 580 S.E.2d 869 (W. Va. 2003), *Frymier-Halloran v. Paige*, 458 S.E.2d 780 (W. Va. 1995), and *State ex rel. Barker v. Manchin*, 279 S.E.2d 622 (W. Va. 1981): This trio of cases explains the separation of powers analysis between the three branches of state government.

- *State ex rel. Smith v. Gore*, 143 S.E.2d 791 (W. Va. 1965): This case has significance on three levels. First, its specific holding—that *all* apportionments for West Virginia elections and public votes must be on the basis of equal population—is a cornerstone of West Virginia govern-

---

14. *Pauley*, 255 S.E.2d at 878.

ment. Second, its application of that principle to, and consequent invalidation of, an apportionment for electing delegates to a constitutional convention thwarted the momentum for creating a new and modern West Virginia Constitution. (Instead, the state adopted several modernizing amendments between 1968 and 1974.) Third, the majority opinion in the case by Justice Caplan demonstrates acumen in the use of tools of constitutional interpretation.

V. Free Online Sources for the West Virginia Constitution

The full text of the West Virginia Constitution is available on the West Virginia Legislature's website.[15] This online version contains an index and a search engine, but also is easily searchable through your computer's "Control F" function.

VI. Print Version of the United States Constitution

The West Virginia Constitution is included in the West Virginia Code sets published by Michie's and West. Research using those sources is explained in Chapter 4.

VII. The West Virginia Constitution on Lexis and Westlaw

The West Virginia Constitution is also available on Lexis and Westlaw with a subscription. Instructions on how to find the Constitution on each site are included in Table 3-2. Of course, on Lexis Advance and WestlawNext, a search using the general search bar may include results from the Constitution.

VIII. The United States Constitution

A. An Overview

While federal constitutional law is a subject worthy of far more words than this short section will allow, researchers may benefit from a brief overview.

---

15. The address is http://www.legis.state.wv.us/wvcode/wv_con.cfm.

Table 3-2. Finding the West Virginia Constitution on Lexis and Westlaw

Lexis Advance	WestlawNext
1. Select "Explore Content" tab 2. Select "West Virginia" under the State tab 3. Select "WV-West Virginia Constitution" under Statutes & Legislation	1. Select the "State Materials" tab 2. Select "West Virginia" 3. Select "West Virginia Statutes and Court Rules" 4. Select "The Constitution of West Virginia (1872)"

Generally, research issues stemming from the federal Constitution hinge on interpretation and implementation of Constitutional provisions. Like the state constitution, the federal Constitution addresses fundamental societal relationships. The federal Constitution covers dealings among the states, interactions between the states and the federal government, the roles of the executive, legislative, and judicial branches, and the rights of the individual with respect to both federal and state governments. Because the United States Supreme Court has played a crucial role in interpreting the Constitution, federal constitutional law researchers rely heavily on Supreme Court decisions.

Further, just as the West Virginia Constitution is divided into Articles that establish the branches of government and enumerate their powers, the United States Constitution takes a similar approach. Table 3-3 lists the Articles and Amendments of the United States Constitution along with a brief description of each Article and Amendment.

Article I establishes the House of Representatives and the Senate. Section 8 of this Article enumerates Congressional powers and includes the well-known "Commerce Clause." Congress has relied on this clause both to regulate commerce with foreign nations and to enact broad federal legislation that affects all states. Section Nine of Article I prohibits Congress from taking certain actions; Section 10 of Article I lists specific actions that individual states are forbidden from taking.

Article II of the Constitution establishes the presidency and the executive branch of government. The powers of the President are not as clearly enumerated as those of the Congress, but Section One vests the President with "executive" power. Section Two establishes the President's role as "commander in chief" and grants the power to pardon. Section Three outlines the President's treaty-making powers and the right to nominate Supreme Court justices and all other federal officers.

Table 3-3. Articles and Amendments of the United States Constitution

Article I	The Legislative Branch
Article II	The Executive Branch
Article III	The Judicial Branch
Article IV	The States
Article V	The Amendment Process
Article VI	Legal Status of the Constitution
Article VII	Ratification
Amendment I	Religion, Speech, Press, Assembly, Petition
Amendment II	Right to Bear Arms
Amendment III	Quartering of Troops
Amendment IV	Searches and Seizures
Amendment V	Grand Jury, Double Jeopardy, Self-Incrimination, Due Process
Amendment VI	Criminal Prosecutions — Jury Trial, Right to Confront and to Counsel
Amendment VII	Common Law Suits — Jury Trial
Amendment VIII	Excess Bail or Fines, Cruel and Unusual Punishment
Amendment IX	Non-Enumerated Rights
Amendment X	Rights Reserved to States or People
Amendment XI	Suits Against a State
Amendment XII	Election of President and Vice-President
Amendment XIII	Abolition of Slavery
Amendment XIV	Privileges and Immunities, Due Process, Equal Protection, Apportionment of Representatives, Civil War Disqualification and Debt
Amendment XV	Rights Not to be Denied on Account of Race
Amendment XVI	Income Tax
Amendment XVII	Popular Election of Senators
Amendment XVIII	Prohibition [Repealed]
Amendment XIX	Women's Right to Vote
Amendment XX	Presidential Term and Succession
Amendment XXI	Repeal of Prohibition Amendment
Amendment XXII	Limitation on Presidential Terms
Amendment XXIII	Presidential Electors for District of Columbia
Amendment XXIV	Poll Tax
Amendment XXV	Presidential Succession
Amendment XXVI	Right to Vote at Age 18
Amendment XXVII	Compensation of Members of Congress

Article III covers the role of the Supreme Court and the rest of the judicial branch of the federal government. The first section of Article IV contains the "Full Faith and Credit Clause," which provides that each state must recognize the public laws, records, and judicial proceedings of the other states.

Article V of the Constitution provides the procedures for amending the Constitution. Including the first ten amendments to the Constitution, commonly known as the Bill of Rights, the Constitution has been amended twenty-seven times. Article VI contains the "Supremacy Clause," which essentially establishes the Constitution as the "Supreme Law of the Land." Furthermore, all federal, state, and local officials must take an oath not to pass laws that interfere with the Constitution, laws passed by Congress, or treaties. In the landmark Supreme Court case of *McCulloch v. Maryland*, the Constitution was interpreted to give the Supreme Court the power to invalidate state actions that interfere with it.[16]

Despite these sweeping provisions, the power of the federal government is not absolute. The Tenth Amendment specifically states that "[t]he powers not delegated to the United States by the Constitution, nor prohibited by it to the states, are reserved to the states respectively, or to the people."[17]

Specific provisions of the Constitution protect individuals from governmental interference. The Bill of Rights provides checks on the federal government's powers, establishing fundamental individual rights such as the rights of free speech, press, and assembly. The Thirteenth Amendment made slavery illegal. The Fourteenth Amendment established due process rights, which have been interpreted by the Supreme Court as affording citizens protection from interference by the state with almost all of the rights listed in the first eight amendments. The exceptions are the right to bear arms in the Second Amendment, the Fifth Amendment guarantee of a grand jury in criminal prosecutions, and the right to a jury for a civil trial under the Seventh Amendment. The Fourteenth Amendment also guarantees equal protection.

The right to vote is protected by several independent amendments, including the 15th Amendment (banning race requirements), the 19th Amendment (forbidding gender restrictions), and the 24th Amendment (establishing the right for citizens age 18 and older).

---

16. *McCulloch v. Maryland*, 17 U.S. 316 (1819).
17. U.S. Const. amend. X.

Table 3-4. Finding the United States Constitution on Lexis and Westlaw

Lexis Advance	WestlawNext
Select "Browse Sources" tab	Select the "Federal Materials" tab
Enter "U.S. Federal" bar	Select "United States Code Annotated"
Select "Statutes and Legislation" under "Content Type"	Select "Constitution of the United States"
Select "USCS — Constitution of the United States"	

B. Free Online Sources for the United States Constitution

The United States Constitution can be found online through Cornell University Law School's Legal Information Institute.[18]

C. Print Version of the United States Constitution

The United States Constitution is included in the West Virginia Code sets published by Michie's and West.

D. The United States Constitution on Lexis and Westlaw

Table 3-4 explains the process for finding the Constitution via Lexis and Westlaw.

IX. Citing Constitutions

Details on citation form for constitutions appear in Chapter 10, but here are two examples (one state case, one federal case) for quick reference:

- West Virginia: W. Va. Const. art. III, §13
- Federal: U.S. Const. art. I, §9

---

18. The address is http://www.law.cornell.edu/constitution.

X. Additional Resources

Robert M. Bastress, Jr., *Constitutional Considerations for Local Government Reform in West Virginia*, 108 W. Va. L. Rev. 125 (2005).

Robert M. Bastress, Jr., *Localism and the West Virginia Constitution*, 109 W. Va. L. Rev. 683 (2006).

Robert M. Bastress, Jr., *The West Virginia State Constitution: A Reference Guide* (1995).

Legal Information Institute
http://www.law.cornell.edu/constitution

Patrick C. McGinley, *Separation of Powers, State Constitutions & the Attorney General: Who Represents the State?*, 99 W. Va. L. Rev. 721 (1996).

Chapter Four

Researching West Virginia Statutory Law and Legislative History

I. Introduction to Statutory Law

While legislative history research was once the most daunting of legal research feats (requiring advanced cross-referencing skills and a heavy dose of patience), technology has changed the game. In fact, it is easier than ever to monitor legislation on its trip to becoming statutory law, with commercial services providing straightforward tracking of each bill's path through the legislative process. Legislative history matters because lawyers can make arguments regarding legislative intent by referencing reports and testimony as well as by tracking the changes that have occurred throughout a bill's journey to passage.

Laws enacted by the legislative branch are called statutes. The United States Congress passes federal statutes, while the West Virginia Legislature is responsible for state statutes. These laws are published in multiple formats, all of which can be useful to legal researchers.

Immediately after a statute is passed, it appears in the federal or state session laws, a chronological compilation of laws passed during a particular legislative session. The session laws are presented in simple chronological order and are not clustered by topic; therefore, an act about shale safety could follow an act regulating wine production. The session laws contain the official text of the law. Federal session laws are compiled in a set known as *Statutes at Large*; the state session laws appear in books entitled *Acts of the Legislature of West Virginia*.

After statutes are passed, they eventually appear in federal and state codes, which organize laws by subject. The United States Code slots federal laws into 53 subject areas called titles and then further arranges them by numbered sections within each title. The West Virginia Code consists of 64 chapters, each with its own subject heading. The chapters are broken down into articles and sections.

The most popular starting point for statutory research, however, is often an annotated code, which provides not only the actual text of the statute, but also many helpful cross-reference suggestions. Many researchers begin by scouring the annotations (which often appear as footnotes) that follow the verbatim statutory text. Annotations may include the history of the statute, cases that interpret the statute, citations to regulations promulgated under the statute, law review articles about the statute, and other research supplements.

West and LexisNexis each publish annotated versions of both the state and federal codes. The state of West Virginia does not publish an official code, but rather relies on LexisNexis and West. Each publishes an annotated code of West Virginia statutes: *Michie's West Virginia Code Annotated* (LexisNexis) and *West's Annotated Code of West Virginia* (West). For the federal codes, West publishes *United States Code Annotated* and LexisNexis publishes *United States Code Service*. Each publisher provides its own annotations that highlight its own products.

II. Researching Statutory Law

While the common law gets top billing in much of legal education, many practitioners spend their careers immersed in statutory research. Statutes, of course, are key primary sources. While some subject areas rest mostly on common law, others are heavily affected by legislative activities. Statutes can preempt earlier decisions, sometimes inadvertently, and sometimes as a result of deliberative legislative action. For example, if the West Virginia Legislature disagrees with an opinion of the West Virginia Supreme Court, it can enact a new statute or amend an existing statute to clarify the contested issue. Conversely, under the system of checks and balances inherent in American law, courts can declare statutes to be unconstitutional if they exceed the authority given to the legislature or conflict with other constitutional provisions.

A word of caution to newer researchers: There are two "codes" in West Virginia—one statutory, one regulatory. Though both are called codes, this chapter focuses on legislation passed by the state legislature that ultimately appears in the statutory code, not regulations passed by administrative agencies (discussed in detail in Chapter 6).

A. West Virginia Code

The West Virginia state statutes appear in two annotated print volumes: *Michie's West Virginia Code Annotated* and *West's Annotated Code of West Virginia*. If you have access to both versions, consult each one, as each publisher will provide unique references to additional authorities in the annotations.

1. *Michie's Code* and Related Services

In the Michie's version of the West Virginia Code, the statutes are arranged by chapter, article, and section. If you don't have a citation to the relevant code section, start with the index volumes, which are typically placed at the end of the set in the law library. The index books are arranged alphabetically and will help you identify your desired statute. Once you have identified the statute by chapter, article, and section, consult the spines of the hardbound volumes; these contain the volume numbers and chapters contained within. Inside the front cover of each volume, you will find a chapter outline. The volumes are updated with pocket parts annually after the legislative session concludes.

Michie's also offers an *Advance Legislative Service*, which contains new acts passed by the legislature that haven't yet been incorporated into the *Acts of the Legislature.* Furthermore, Michie's provides the *Advanced Code Service*, which comes out shortly after the legislative sessions are over and is updated cumulatively three times per year with new annotations. It is published before the annual full pocket part update to alert readers of changes because it takes time for the full pocket part updates to be produced.

Finally, Michie's offers a *Legislative Review Service*, which contains summaries of significant new laws of interest. It comes out once per year and is organized by subject.

2. *West's West Virginia Code* and Related Services

The second published set of West Virginia's statutes, *West's Annotated Code of West Virginia*, also is arranged by chapter, article, and section. Like the Michie's version, this annotated code contains an alphabetical index that can lead you to the desired code section. On the spine, you will find the volume number and the chapters contained within.

West publishes pocket parts once per year, after the legislative sessions. If the pocket part gets too large and unwieldy, West will publish a softbound pocket part called a supplementary pamphlet.

West also publishes the *West Virginia Legislative Service*, which contains new acts passed by the legislature but not yet incorporated into the *Acts of the Leg-*

Table 4-1. Accessing the West Virginia Code Online

West Virginia Legislature	1. Access by: http://www.legis.state.wv.us/wvcode/code.cfm 2. Search by reviewing the table of contents or conducting a full text search
WestlawNext	1. Choose the "Statutes and Court Rules" Tab 2. Click "West Virginia"
Lexis Advance	1. Choose "Statutes and Legislation" under the "Content Type" tab 2. Choose "West Virginia" under the "Jurisdiction" tab or 1. Search "WV — West Virginia Code" in search bar 2. Click "WV — West Virginia Code" under "Content Type"

islature. Furthermore, West offers an *Interim Update Service*, which comes out shortly after the legislative sessions. It is published before the annual full pocket part update to alert readers of changes.

As with most legal resources, the online versions of the state statutes are updated much more frequently than print volumes, and are often the easiest to use. Table 4-1 shows the various entry points for online researchers to access the West Virginia Code.

Figure 4-1 offers a framework for approaching statutory law research in West Virginia.

Figure 4-1. Researching West Virginia Statutory Law

Do you know the relevant code section?	If you do not have a relevant statute,	
If so, look it up in either Michie's Annotated Code or West's Annotated Code. These volumes provide annotations that cross-reference important primary sources, including cases and regulations that interpret or apply the statute.	**create a list of search terms.** You may wish to begin with Michie's Jurisprudence to gain background knowledge on your subject. Also, these secondary sources will lead you to primary sources that interpret the statute.	**Look to legislative history if you need further clarification on legislative intent.**

B. The *United States Code*

Just as West Virginia's statutes are codified, the statutes passed by the United States Congress eventually wind up in a code organized by subject matter. The official *United States Code* (U.S.C.) contains 53 separately numbered titles; each title holds laws relating to the subject of the particular volume. Because the sections are indexed and organized by subject, you can find laws even if you don't know exactly when they were passed. Citations include a title number (subject category) and section number. For instance, 26 U.S.C. 112 indicates that the information can be found in title 26 and section 112 of the *United States Code*. The Code is revised every year six years with annual supplements published in hardbound volumes. The supplements contain revisions from the prior year and updated tables.

Two commercial publishers provide annotated versions of the United States Code: the *United States Code Annotated* (West) and the *United States Code Service* (LexisNexis). Both provide the statutory text as well as references to cases and regulations that interpret the statute; they are updated more frequently with pocket part supplements and almost immediately in online versions. As with the *United States Code*, both titles have multi-volume indexes and volumes with supplemental tables.

III. Introduction to the Legislative Process

When lawyers talk about legislative history, they are referring to the events that precipitated a statute's enactment. While the historical record of how federal statutes come to fruition is often quite robust, in West Virginia, legislative history may be hard to come by. That being said, you may be able to find legislative history in the form of transcripts of hearings, committee reports, and sometimes transcripts or summaries of floor debates. Lawyers sometimes need to consult these historical documents to uncover the intent behind a statute—or to make an argument in support of a particular interpretation.

A. How a West Virginia Bill Becomes a Law

Anyone can propose an idea for a bill to a member of the West Virginia Assembly—the sources range from private citizens to special interest groups to governmental units. But all bills need sponsorship to be considered by the Legislature. (In the House, the number of sponsors of a bill or a constitutional amendment is limited to seven delegates while the Senate has no limit on sponsorship.)

Initially, some bills are reviewed by the state's Office of Legislative Services or legislative staff counsel to ensure proper form. After the draft legislation is prepared, the legislator reviews it and submits it to the clerk of the chamber of which he or she is a member. Prior to the bill's formal introduction, the clerk assigns a bill number, which is used as the bill's reference throughout the legislative session.

After the bill is numbered, the President of the Senate or the Speaker of the House of Delegates assigns the bill to a committee or committees to be considered. When the bill is formally introduced on the floor of the chamber, the bill number and the committee references are announced.

The bill next enters the committee study phase of the legislative process. Standing Committees are small groups of senators or delegates assigned to study bills. This process enables a larger number of bills to receive more detailed study than can be done by the entire House or Senate.

When a committee has completed work on a bill, it files a written committee report that recommends passage (with or without amendment or substitute) or rejection, or it can remain silent. A bill can "die in committee," meaning the committee did not have enough time to take up the issue or the members decided that the bill should not be recommended to the full membership for action.

Once a bill is out of committee, the committee's recommendation for that legislation is read on the floor of the House or Senate. The Rules Committee of each chamber then determines which bills will be considered. Those bills are slotted on the House or Senate daily calendar, which lists all bills to be acted on in each chamber. The calendar of bills to be acted on is divided into bills on first reading, bills on second reading, and bills on third reading.

Under the West Virginia Constitution, a bill must be read three times.[1] The first reading of the bill alerts the membership of each chamber that the bill will be considered. On second reading, members vote on the committee's amendments. The vote on the bill's passage occurs at the third reading.

---

1. W. Va. Const. art. VI, § 29.

If a bill is passed by one chamber, either House or Senate, it is sent to the other body, where it will be referred to committee and the process is repeated.

If changes are made in a bill by the second chamber, it must be sent back to the first chamber for its concurrence. If the first chamber does not agree and the second chamber refuses to remove the changes it made, a conference committee with an equal number of representatives from both chambers is appointed by the Senate President and House Speaker to work out the differences in the bill.

If this committee reaches a compromise, the bill is considered for a vote once again. If a compromise is not reached, then another conference committee may be appointed, or the measure will die in committee when the Legislature adjourns.

After a bill passes both chambers in the same form, it is sent to the Governor. While the Legislature is in session, the Governor has five days to approve or veto the bill. After the Legislature adjourns, the Governor has 15 days to act on most bills. However, the budget bill and supplemental appropriations bills must be acted upon by the Governor within five days regardless of when they are received. If the Governor does not act within these time limits, the bill automatically becomes a law.

If the Legislature is still in session when the Governor vetoes a bill, a simple majority vote of the members of both legislative bodies is necessary to override the veto. In cases when a budget bill or supplemental appropriation bill is vetoed, a two-thirds vote of the members of both chambers is needed to override the veto.

Table 4-2 illustrates the legislative process in West Virginia.

B. Records of the Legislative Process in West Virginia

The West Virginia Legislature produces very little documentation of its legislative process. In general, the only widely available background documents are the various drafts of House and Senate bills and the summary proceedings and bill histories contained in the *Journal of the House of Delegates* and the *Journal of the Senate.*

Table 4-2. West Virginia's Legislative Process

Bill gets introduced by a member of the House or Senate

Bill gets referred to a committee by the House Speaker or Senate President

The committee considers the bill

The committee reports the bill to the members of the House or Senate

It is read a first time, amended, and then read a second time

It is read a third time and members of the House or Senate debate and vote on the bill

If passed, the bill is sent to the second chamber where the process repeats

If passed by the second chamber, the bill is signed into law or vetoed by the Governor

Legislature may vote to override the veto, and the bill becomes law without the Governor's approval

Table 4-3 lists potential sources of West Virginia legislative history and their attributes.

C. Steps to Compiling Legislative History for a West Virginia Statute

1. Book Approach

Legislative history research — particularly in the books — can be painstaking; don't be afraid to ask for help if the task gets overwhelming. Because the entirety of West Virginia's session laws are not yet freely available online, sometimes the cumbersome book research process is the only route. The key to finding the relevant history of a statutory provision is the bill number. The process follows these general steps: (1) look to the statute to find the chapter number,

Table 4-3. Potential Sources for West Virginia Legislative History

Journal of the House of Delegates and the *Journal of the Senate*	• Printed daily, available online • Contains the official record of the proceedings that take place each day while the House of Delegates/ Senate is in session • Follows the Order of Business and details floor actions on any legislation up for introduction, amendment or passage • Includes results of all roll call votes • May include verbatim remarks that a legislator has requested to be included
Committee Reports	• When bills are referred to committees within the Senate or House for their opinions on bill approval, a report is created and generally consists of only one or two sentence statements addressing the bill
Audio for Floor Sessions and Public Hearings	• Certain House or Senate floor sessions and public hearings are available on the West Virginia Legislature's website

year of enactment, and session; (2) take that information and consult the *Acts of the Legislature of West Virginia* for that year and session to find the bill number; (3) locate the bill number in either the *Journal of the House of Delegates* or the *Journal of the Senate* in order to locate page numbers in those journals for major actions; (4) review the materials on those pages with respect to major actions and other proceedings with respect to that bill number.

More specifically, if you are using book resources to research the history of a West Virginia statute, start by determining the chapter number that created or amended the relevant section and the particular year and legislative session (regular or extraordinary) in which the legislature enacted the chapter. The chapter, year, and session references are located immediately following the end of the code section in the parenthetical information. For example, the parenthetical at the end of W. Va. Code Ann. § 61-10-22 (addressing Bribery of Participants in Professional or Amateur Games or Horseracing) cites "Acts 1945, c. 45." This reference indicates that the bill that was eventually codified in W. Va. Code Ann. § 61-10-22 was enacted during the regular session of the Legislature in 1945, and that it can be found in Chapter 45 of the *Acts of the Legislature of West Virginia*.

Figure 4-2. Example from *Acts of the Legislature of West Virginia*

---o---

CHAPTER 45

(Senate Bill No. 149 — By Mr. Hardesty and Mr. Harmer)

AN ACT to amend article ten, chapter sixty-one of the code of West Virginia, one thousand nine hundred thirty-one, by adding thereto a new section, to be numbered section twenty-two, relating to bribery of participants in games, sports and horse racing, and providing penalties.

[Passed March 10, 1945: in effect ninety days from passage. Approved by the Governor.]

Article 10. Crimes Against Public Policy.

Section

22. Bribery of participants in professional or amateur games and horse racing.

Be it enacted by the Legislature of West Virginia:

That article ten, chapter sixty-one of the code of West Virginia, one thousand nine hundred thirty-one, be amended by adding thereto a new section, to be numbered section twenty-two, to read as follows:

　　Section 22. *Bribery of Participants in Professional or*
2　*Amateur Games and Horse Racing.*—Whoever gives, prom-
3　ises or offers to any professional or amateur baseball,
4　football, basketball, hockey player or boxer or any player
5　who participates in any professional or amateur game or

Once you have determined the relevant year, session, and chapter number, you need to consult the volume of the *Acts of the Legislature of West Virginia* for that year and session. The chapters are arranged in numerical order within each session. The House or Senate bill number attached to the bill during the legislative process will be listed just below the chapter number and before the text of the act. For example, Chapter 45, cited above, is derived from Senate Bill No. 149 (see Figure 4-2 above). You will also find the sponsor or sponsors of the bill listed below the bill number.

Once you have determined the relevant bill number, it is time to consult the House and Senate journals. The bill history tables for the *Journal of the*

House of Delegates are found at the end of the volume or volumes produced for that year's session. The bill history tables for the *Journal of the Senate* are located immediately before the text of the first day of the regular session and before each extraordinary session that may have occurred in that year.

Each journal's bill history table contains separate sequences for the House bills that were considered and the Senate bills that were considered during a particular session. The bill history tables list page numbers within that journal for major actions such as (1) the introduction of a bill, (2) reporting a bill out of committee, (3) amending the text of a bill, and (4) passage of a bill from a chamber. Another list of page numbers are listed under the heading "Other Proceedings," which include more routine actions such as "first reading" of a bill (i.e., the text of the introduced bill is read to the chamber) and activities such as a message presenting a House-passed bill to the Senate or vice-versa.

Once you have determined the page numbers for major actions that have been taken on the bill, consult those pages. For a complete search, the page numbers under "Other Proceedings" also should be examined. It is important to note that the House and Senate journals are primarily useful for determining what happened to a bill and when that action took place. For the most part, the journals simply describe the proceedings of the legislature and other than the language of amendments, the journals do not contain textual materials such as the full text of bills, substantive committee reports, or floor debates.

2. Online Approach

a. West Virginia Legislature

The West Virginia Legislature's website provides access to the full text of bills, and their histories, from 1993 to date.[2] Bill histories list all actions taken on a bill in chronological order. Bills and bill histories can be located by clicking on the link to "Bill Status" from the opening screen of the website and then selecting the year and session. Bills can be located by bill number, sponsor, and subject category.

By clicking on "Bulletin Board" from the opening screen, researchers can access the full text of the daily legislative journals, arranged by date and day of the session. The House journals are available from 2003 to date and the Senate journals are available from 2005 to date.

By clicking on "Bill Status" and then "Bill Tracking," researchers can create a "personalized bill tracking" account to be able to track legislation that is currently before the Legislature.

---

2. The address is http://www.legis.state.wv.us.

b. Lexis Advance

In order to find West Virginia legislative history resources on Lexis Advance, under "Explore Content," choose the "State" tab and then "West Virginia" as the jurisdiction, and then click on "All West Virginia Statutes & Legislation" under the "Statutes & Legislation" menu. You can then search within all the available legislative history materials on Lexis Advance via the "Legislative History" tab.

You can also locate legislative history by searching for a statute and then clicking "Go to" followed by "History." Acts of the Legislature are available beginning in 1989 on Lexis Advance.

c. WestlawNext

To locate West Virginia legislative history resources on WestlawNext, choose "State Materials" and then choose "West Virginia Statutes & Court Rules," search for the statute, and then click on the "History" tab. This leads you to reports and journals related to the statute.

Acts of the Legislature are available beginning in 1990.

d. Bloomberg Law

To locate West Virginia legislative sources on Bloomberg Law, from the "Browse All Content" page, click on "Laws & Regulations" and then "State Laws & Regulations." Choose "West Virginia" from the map and then "W. Va. Legislative." Bloomberg's coverage for Acts dates back to December 1998.

IV. Statutory and Legislative History Citation

A. Citing Statutes

The rules for citing statutes are a bit complicated and vary depending upon which specific source you consult. Generally, Bluebook citation form for the West Virginia Code Annotated requires the following:

- W. Va. Code Ann. § chapter-article-section (publisher and year)

Examples:

- W. Va. Code Ann. § 42-1-3 (LexisNexis 2010)

- W. Va. Code Ann. § 42-1-3 (West 2002)

However, the parenthetical information depends upon which version you consult. When citing a bound (book) version of the code, use the year located on the spine.

Example:

- W. Va. Code Ann. § 46-4-202 (LexisNexis 2007).

If the statute has been updated and the updates appear in the pocket part, the date you provide in the parenthetical depends upon the information cited. A section that was added after the bound version of the code was published and that is published entirely in the pocket part would be cited as follows:

- W. Va. Code Ann. § 46-9-808 (LexisNexis Supp. 2012).

However, when citing a section of the code that appears in both the bound volume of the code and the pocket part, the citation requires reference to both the bound volume and the pocket part publication dates:

- W. Va. Code Ann. § 46-9-625 (LexisNexis 2007 & Supp. 2012).

Citations to the United States Code are a bit more straightforward. Even though you may use the annotated versions for research, the Bluebook requires citation to the official United States Code, as follows:

- title number U.S.C. § section (year)

Example:

- 42 U.S.C. § 1983 (2006)

The United States Code is published every six years. As of this printing, the latest version of the United States Code available was published in 2006. If material in the official United States Code appears in the pocket part, the citation's parenthetical would include the date on the spine of the book, an ampersand ("&"), Supp., and the date of the supplement.

Example:

- 42 U.S.C. § 7256 (2006 & Supp. I 2012).

B. Citing Legislative History

Once a bill is enacted, the Bluebook prefers a citation strictly to the statute. However, you may need to cite to bills that have been enacted when documenting legislative history. You also may need to cite bills that were not enacted for historical purposes. Examples of how to cite bills that were not enacted and those that were enacted are as follows:

West Virginia Bills (not enacted):

- H.B. 2589, 83rd Leg., Reg. Sess. (W. Va. 2017).

- S.B. 441, 83rd Leg., Reg. Sess. (W. Va. 2017).

West Virginia Bills (enacted):

- S.B. 225, 2017 Leg., Reg. Sess., 2017 W. Va. Acts 65.

- H.B. 2815, 2017 Leg. Reg. Sess., 2017 W. Va. Acts 122.

Federal Bills (not enacted):

- H.R. 3762, 114th Cong. (2016).

- S. 1, 114th Cong. (2015).

Federal Bills (enacted)

- H.R. 4374, 115th Cong. (2017).

- S. 1866, 115th Cong. (2017).

Rule B13 in the blue pages of the *Bluebook* appears to make no distinction between federal bills that were enacted and those that were not enacted. However, Rule 13.2 in the white pages of the *Bluebook* suggests that for concurrent resolutions, *Statutes at Large,* and for single resolutions, a citation to the *Congressional Record* may be provided if it would assist the reader. However, it is sufficient to note that the resolution was enacted in a parenthetical, as follows:

Federal Bills (enacted):

- H.R. Res. 458, 115th Cong. (2017) (enacted).

V. Additional Resources

Citizen's Guide to the Legislature
    http://www.legis.state.wv.us/Educational/citizens/process.cfm

Congressional Website
    https://www.congress.gov

House of Delegates Committees
www.wvlegislature.gov/committees/house/main.cfm

How a Bill Becomes a Law (West Virginia Legislature)
http://www.legis.state.wv.us/Educational/Bill_Becomes_Law/Bill_
Becomes_Law.cfm

Legislative Bulletin Board (*contains bills to be introduced by both Senate and
the House, bill histories, Senate and House calendars, and the journals of
both the Senate and House*)
http://www.legis.state.wv.us/Bulletin_Board/Bulletin_Board_menu.cfm

Senate Committees
www.wvlegislature.gov/committees/senate/main.cfm

United States Code via Law Library of Congress
http://www.loc.gov/collections/united-states-code/

West Virginia Bill Tracking
www.wvlegislature.gov/billstatus_personalized/PBT/persbills_login.cfm

West Virginia Code
code.wvlegislature.gov

West Virginia "Helpful Links"
www.wvlegislature.gov/Contact/Links/links.cfm

West Virginia Legislature's Bill Drafting Manual
www.wvlegislature.gov/legisdocs/misc/pub/Drafting_Manual.pdf

West Virginia Legislature Live
www.wvlegislature.gov/live.cfm

West Virginia Office of Reference and Information
www.wvlegislature.gov/Joint/legisinfo.cfm

Chapter Five

Researching West Virginia Case Law

I. Introduction to Case Law Research

A. Understanding Cases

Law students know cases—they spend years reading textbooks full of them. But once legal researchers are working outside of the academic setting, they sometimes forget that a combination of legal resources may be needed to provide a supervisor with all of the applicable "rules" on a legal topic. While law students spend the great majority of their time working with cases, practitioners often combine cases with other legal authorities to provide a comprehensive explanation of the law. For example, initial searching may point a legal researcher to a statute or constitutional provision, but cases interpreting those sources would also be needed to fully explain the law. This chapter will teach you how to find cases and use them effectively.

Written decisions issued by courts are commonly referred to as cases, judicial opinions, or decisions. Cases are compiled in print volumes called reporters or case reports. While not as voluminous as in the pre-digital age, reporters still absorb quite a bit of real estate in a law library.

But finding the cases that round out your legal research is not as simple as pulling a reporter off a shelf. Even in the electronic era, case law research can be grueling, largely because it is not easy to determine when you have located the "best" cases. The case law research process can be approached from multiple angles, and in this chapter, you will learn a variety of techniques to discover the cases you need.

First things first: effective case law researchers focus on jurisdiction early in the process. A fishing analogy is apropos. Imagine that all case law possibilities are contained in one of two ponds; one is labeled "federal" and one is labeled "state." Then, ask yourself which pond contains the fish you need. Inexperienced researchers often flub research tasks early by "fishing in the wrong pond." If your supervisor expects West Virginia cases and you deliver federal authority, you have not satisfied her request. Moreover, fishing in one giant pond labeled "federal and state" will yield species that confuse your supervisor.

After you feel confident that you've located cases from the desired jurisdiction, the hierarchy of authority comes into play. Federal courts and state courts follow a similar hierarchical organization: trial courts at the bottom, appellate courts in the middle, and highest courts at the top. Higher-level courts publish their decisions in chronological order in official case reporters; some lower-level decisions are available in case reporters, but some are not. As the digital revolution takes hold, researchers can expect more content to be found online and less in books, as governments looking to cut costs are increasingly turning to electronic publishing as a cost-saving measure.

Pay close attention to the level of court that issues a decision that you are considering citing, as that will determine whether the case will be either binding or merely persuasive to other courts. Mandatory precedent is just what its name implies—it is binding and must be followed. Persuasive precedent, on the other hand, might persuade a court to follow suit, but it might not.

A decision made by a higher-level court in the hierarchy, or by the same court in an earlier decision, is binding precedent that the court itself and all its inferior courts must follow. The principle of stare decisis holds that a court should not overturn its own precedent unless there is a strong reason to do so.

Persuasive precedent can include cases decided by lower courts, cases decided by peer or higher courts from other geographic jurisdictions, cases issued in parallel systems, and even statements made in dicta, treatises, or law review articles.

You can find case law in many ways. Commercial entities, such as Lexis and Westlaw, publish cases in book form and online. Subscription services such as Fastcase offer all members of the state bar access to a limited library of cases. And of course, many cases are freely available via a variety of websites, including individual court web pages.

B. A Note on Unpublished or Non-Precedential Opinions

Not all cases are published; if a court determines that its opinion does not add to the existing precedent in the jurisdiction, the court may decline to officially publish it. But even "unpublished" cases may prove valuable to legal researchers, who may come across cases that are marked "not designated for publication" through an online search. For example, unpublished opinions can be good sources for finding references to published cases.

While lawyers generally prefer not to rely on unpublished cases, a relatively recent addition to the Federal Rules of Appellate Procedure make clear that unpublished opinions can be cited in documents submitted to federal courts.[1]

II. Understanding Court Systems

A. West Virginia Court Structure

1. Introduction

The process of finding case law requires an understanding of both the state and federal court systems and the hierarchy of authority within each system.

Like all systems, West Virginia has a high court at the top of the pyramid: the West Virginia Supreme Court of Appeals. (Note: West Virginia lawyers often use the terms West Virginia Supreme Court of Appeals and West Virginia Supreme Court interchangeably.) And like most state courts, the base of the system is broad, with a variety of lower-level courts providing the first point of access to the court system. (Examples include Family Court and Magistrate Court.) However, unlike many other states, West Virginia does not have an intermediate court of appeals. Thus, the path from trial court to the state's court of last resort is relatively short. That being said, the jurisdiction of the West Virginia Supreme Court of Appeals is purely discretionary, and it is quite unusual in that regard. West Virginia jurisprudence holds that appellate review is not essential so long as due process has been accorded at the trial level. Accordingly, the West Virginia Supreme Court may grant or refuse review of any case.

Table 5-1 provides a visual depiction of the courts operating in West Virginia.

2. West Virginia Supreme Court of Appeals

a. Introduction

The Supreme Court of Appeals is West Virginia's court of last resort. Because West Virginia is one of only nine states with a single appellate court (and no intermediate court to ease its burden), the Supreme Court of Appeals of West Virginia is one of the busiest appellate courts of its type in the country.[2]

---

1. Fed. R. App. P. 32.1.
2. http://courtswv.gov/public-resources/press/Publications/2016_CourtBrochure.
pdf.

Table 5-1. Courts of West Virginia

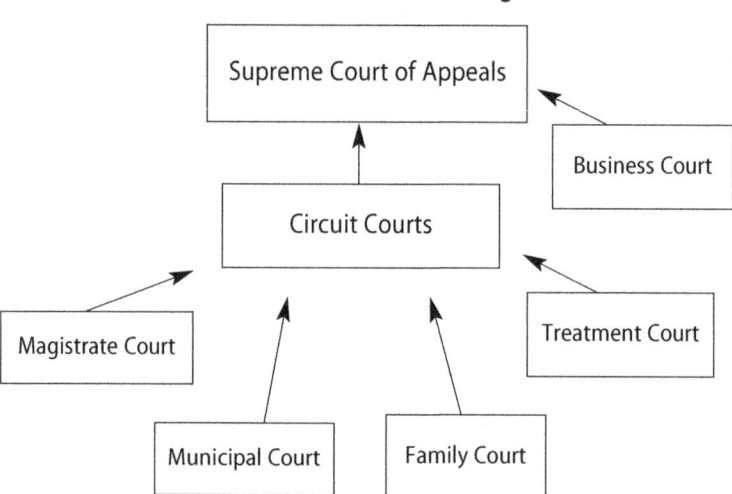

The five Supreme Court justices hear appeals from administrative agencies and from the circuit courts, including criminal convictions affirmed on appeal from Magistrate Court. Under West Virginia law, workers' compensation claims are appealed directly to the Supreme Court from the administrative agency. The Supreme Court justices also hear appeals from Family Court decisions if both parties agree that they will not appeal directly to the circuit court.

The justices hold extraordinary writ powers and possess original jurisdiction in proceedings involving habeas corpus, mandamus, prohibition, and certiorari. They also interpret the laws and Constitutions of West Virginia and the United States.

b. Syllabus Points

Another peculiarity in West Virginia law is the syllabus and syllabus point. In essence, the West Virginia Supreme Court writes a set of introductory notes (also known as the syllabus) that precedes the text of the opinion. These points of law—essentially a collection of the case's key holdings—are frequently referred to by the West Virginia Supreme Court in subsequent opinions and are considered to be binding and quite influential. The West Virginia Constitution requires the Court to draft syllabus points for every written opinion in which the majority of the justices concur.[3] These syllabus points written by the Court

---

3. "[I]t shall be the duty of the court to prepare a syllabus of the points adjudicated in each case in which an opinion is written and in which a majority of the justices

Figure 5-1. Syllabus Point Example

**512 *277 Syllabus by the Court

1. "Contributory negligence and assumption of risk are not identical. The essence of contributory negligence is carelessness; of assumption of risk, venturousness. Knowledge and appreciation of the danger are necessary elements of assumption of risk. Failure to use due care under the circumstances constitutes the element of contributory negligence." Syllabus Point 5, *Spurlin v. Nardo*, 145 W.Va. 408, 114 S.E.2d 913 (1960).

2. A plaintiff is not barred from recovery by the doctrine of assumption of risk unless his degree of fault arising therefrom equals or exceeds the combined fault or negligence of the other parties to the accident.

3. The defense of assumption of risk is available against a plaintiff in a product liability case where it is shown that the plaintiff had actual knowledge of the defective or dangerous condition, fully appreciated the risks involved, and continued to use the product. However, the plaintiff is not barred from recovery unless his degree of fault under assumption of risk equals or exceeds the combined fault of the other parties to the accident.

4. To determine whether to make a new rule of law retroactive, courts consider the following factors: (1) whether the issue involves a settled area of the law where retroactivity would be less justified or a changing area where retroactivity would be more likely and whether the new rule is foreshadowed; (2) procedural rules are more likely to be afforded retroactivity than substantive points; (3) common law **513 *278 rule changes are more likely to be applied retroactively; (4) substantial public policy changes are less likely to be applied retroactively; (5) the more radical the departure from prior law, the less likelihood for retroactivity; and (6) analogous decisions of other jurisdictions.

5. The doctrine of comparative assumption of risk should be made fully retroactive. Consequently, comparative assumption of risk is available in all cases tried after the date of this opinion, including those on retrial. Additionally, it applies on appeal if the point was preserved at trial.

Source: *King v. Kayak Mfg. Corp.*, 387 S.E.2d 511 (W. Va. 1989). Reprinted with permission of West.

should not be confused with the headnotes and other enhancements added by publishers. Those enhancements are covered later in this chapter.

Figure 5-1 contains an example of syllabus points written by the West Virginia Supreme Court.

c. Types of Decisions Issued by the West Virginia
Supreme Court of Appeals

The Supreme Court of Appeals of West Virginia has historically issued four types of court opinions: signed opinions, per curiam opinions, memorandum decisions, and separate opinions or decisions.[4]

Signed opinions are delivered by one justice on behalf of the Court and contain at least one new syllabus point.[5] Signed opinions can be found in the *West Virginia Reports*[6] and the *Southeastern (Second) Reporter.*

---

thereof concurred, which shall be prefixed to the published report of the case." W. Va. Const. art. VIII, § 4.

4. *Appellate Case Types and Decision Types*, West Virginia Judiciary, http://www.courtswv.gov/supreme-court/integrated-decision-list-explained.html (last visited Jan. 25, 2018).

5. *Id.*

6. *Id.*

As of 2014, the Supreme Court of Appeals of West Virginia stopped issuing per curiam opinions, but you will uncover many if you are searching for earlier decisions. Per curiam opinions were opinions delivered by the Court as a whole that did not contain new syllabus points, but rather quoted syllabus points from prior decisions.[7] Per curiam opinions have precedential value in that they apply settled principles to new fact patterns and also help lower courts properly apply syllabus points.[8] Per curiam opinions also appeared in the state[9] and regional reporters.

Memorandum decisions are short decisions on the merits of a case.[10] They do not contain syllabus points, but may be cited as authority in any West Virginia court or administrative tribunal.[11] Memorandum decisions are not found in published reporters,[12] but can be found on the website of the West Virginia Judiciary.[13]

Separate opinions or decisions are written by a justice separately from the majority and explain why the Justice concurs, dissents, or a combination of the two.[14]

At the beginning of each decision issued by the West Virginia Supreme Court, basic information is provided, such as the full name of the case, the court that decided the case, the different citations for each publishing reporter, and the date the case was decided.

The West Virginia Supreme Court then writes its own syllabus, which contains the syllabus points of the major holdings of the case. (See Figure 5-1.) Next, the attorneys representing both parties are listed. Then the opinion begins with the name of the justice writing the opinion. C.J. stands for Chief Justice, J. stands for Justice, and JJ. is the plural for Justices or Judges. The opinion may be broken down into headings. Be sure to check for dissenting or concurring opinions[15] after the majority's opinion.

---

7. *Id.*

8. *Id.*

9. *Id.*

10. *Id.*

11. W. Va. Rev. R. App. P. 21(e).

12. West Virginia Judiciary, *supra* note 5.

13. The address is at http://www.courtswv.gov/supreme-court/opinions.html. Memorandum decisions are abbreviated as "MD."

14. West Virginia Judiciary, *supra* note 5.

15. Generally, a "dissenting opinion" or "dissent" refers to an opinion filed by one or more judges that disagrees with the majority. A "concurring opinion" or "concurrence" refers to an opinion filed by one or more judges that agrees with the result in a case, but under a different rationale.

3. Circuit Courts

The circuit courts are West Virginia's only general jurisdiction trial courts of record. Circuit courts have jurisdiction over all civil cases at law worth more than $2,500 with limited exceptions, and all felonies and misdemeanors. The circuit courts receive appeals from magistrate court, municipal court, and administrative agencies, excluding workers' compensation appeals. The circuit courts also hear appeals of family court decisions unless both parties agree to appeal directly to the Supreme Court of Appeals. The circuit courts receive recommended orders from judicial officers who hear mental hygiene and juvenile matters.

West Virginia's fifty-five counties are divided into thirty-one circuits, with seventy-four circuit judges presiding. The circuits range in size from one circuit with seven judges to nine circuits with one judge. Although as few as one or as many as four counties comprise a circuit, each county has a courthouse where the circuit judge presides.

Since 2016, the West Virginia citizenry has elected circuit judges in nonpartisan elections. Circuit judges must have practiced law for at least five years and are elected to eight-year terms. The Governor appoints circuit judges to fill vacancies, but an appointee who wishes to remain in office must run in the next election.

4. Magistrate Courts

There are 158 magistrates in West Virginia, with at least two sitting in every county. Ten magistrates hear cases in Kanawha County, West Virginia's largest county and home to the state's capital city of Charleston.

Magistrates oversee the application and enforcement of state laws, municipal laws, and court procedures. Magistrates have jurisdiction over civil cases worth less than ten thousand dollars. They hear misdemeanor cases and conduct preliminary examinations in felony cases. In criminal cases, they issue and record affidavits, complaints, arrest warrants, and search warrants. They also set bail and make decisions concerning proposed plea agreements, the collection of courts costs, cash bonds, and fines.

Magistrates issue emergency protective orders in domestic violence cases. They are charged with immediately entering domestic violence petitions into the Domestic Violence Database and Registry.

In some counties where there are no mental hygiene commissioners, the chief judge of the circuit court can designate a magistrate to handle involuntary hospitalization cases. However, magistrates cannot handle final commitment or guardianship cases. In some counties, both mental hygiene commissioners and designated magistrates are appointed by the chief judge to perform portions of the county's mental hygiene work. After hours and on weekends, magistrates can enter mental hygiene orders into West Virginia's Mental Health Registry and issue applications and temporary placement orders.

Magistrates work under the administrative supervision of the Supreme Court of Appeals of West Virginia; their decisions are appealed to one of the state's circuit courts.

5. Municipal Court

West Virginia municipal courts handle DWI/DUI cases, traffic infractions, and parking and ordinance violations.

6. Business Court

The Business Court is a relative newcomer to West Virginia's court system. Legislation to create a business court was first introduced in 2008 and, in 2010, the West Virginia Legislature adopted House Bill 4352, which allowed the state Supreme Court to establish a business court docket within the existing system. The Court seems to be realizing its goal of removing complex commercial cases from the circuit courts and transferring them into a specialized forum, freeing the circuit court dockets to handle less complicated cases more efficiently. The West Virginia Supreme Court of Appeals began accepting transfer requests to the new Business Court in October 2012. By 2017, more than 270 businesses had been involved in litigation in Business Court. Since inception, approximately 60% of cases referred to the Business Court involved contract disputes or alleged tortious business practices, approximately 20% involved complex tax appeals, and the remainder related to complex transactions, operations or governance between business entities, such as shareholder derivative actions, alleged monopolies, mismanagement of trusts, violations of the state's Unfair Trade Practices Act and disputes regarding the scope of easements, rights of way, and restrictive covenants.

7. Family Court

Family Court judges hear cases on the following family law topics: divorce, annulment, separate maintenance, paternity, grandparent visitation, allocation of parental responsibility, and family support. They do not conduct child abuse and neglect proceedings; those cases are handled by the circuit courts. Family court judges also hold final hearings in domestic violence civil proceedings.

Table 5-2. Structure of the Federal Court System

Appellate Courts	Trial Courts	Courts Operating Outside the Judicial Branch
• Includes the U.S. Courts of Appeals • 12 Regional Circuit Courts of Appeals • 1 U.S. Court of Appeals for each Federal Circuit	• Includes the U.S. District Courts • 94 Judicial Districts • Also includes U.S. Bankruptcy Court, U.S. Court of International Trade, and U.S. Court of Federal Claims	• Includes the U.S. Court of Appeals for the Armed Forces (Military Courts), U.S. Court of Appeals for Veterans Claims, and U.S. Tax Court

There are forty-seven family court judges who serve within twenty-seven family court circuits. Family Court judges, who were previously appointed by the Governor, were elected in partisan elections for the first time in 2002. Their initial terms span six years, but subsequent terms last eight years. In 2016, all judicial elections became nonpartisan.

8. Treatment Court

The West Virginia court system continues to add treatment or "problem-solving" courts throughout the state to help participants overcome addictions and mental illnesses that may have led them to commit crimes. Registered sex offenders and criminals with prior convictions for a violent felony are not eligible for treatment court programs. Prosecutors and judges choose which offenders may participate.

There are several types of treatment courts in West Virginia, including adult drug courts and juvenile drug courts.

B. Federal Court Structure

1. Introduction

While the federal court system cannot be thoroughly explained in this short volume, a bit of background may prove useful to researchers. Table 5-2 shows the structure of the federal court system. Note that West Virginia falls within the Fourth Circuit Court of Appeals, along with Maryland, Virginia, North Carolina, and South Carolina.

2. U.S. Supreme Court

Nine members, including a Chief Justice and eight associate justices, comprise the venerable Supreme Court of the United States. At its discretion, the Supreme Court chooses a select group of cases to decide each year, and these cases typically involve important questions about the United States Constitution or federal law.

3. U.S. Courts of Appeals

Thirteen appellate courts sit below the United States Supreme Court, and they are collectively referred to as the Courts of Appeals. The 94 U.S. judicial districts are organized into 12 regional circuits, each of which has a United States Court of Appeals. A court of appeals hears appeals from the district courts located within its circuit, as well as appeals from decisions of federal administrative agencies. In addition, the Court of Appeals for the Federal Circuit has nationwide jurisdiction to hear appeals in specialized cases, such as those involving patent laws and cases decided by the Court of International Trade and the Court of Federal Claims.

Appellate courts do not retry cases or hear evidence; a jury is not present. Instead, appellate courts review trial court procedures and decisions to ensure that the proceedings were just and that the proper law was correctly applied. West Virginia sits in the Fourth Circuit Court of Appeals, located in Richmond, Virginia. Links to opinions, docket information, an argument calendar, rules and procedures, and forms and notices are all available on the court's website.[16]

4. U.S. District Courts

The United States District Courts serve as trial courts in the federal court system. These courts hear nearly all categories of federal cases, including both civil and criminal matters.

There are 94 federal judicial districts, including at least one district in each state and the District of Columbia. Four territories of the United States — Puerto Rico, the Virgin Islands, Guam, and the Northern Mariana Islands — have district courts that hear federal cases, including bankruptcy cases.

Bankruptcy courts operate as separate units of the district courts; federal courts have exclusive jurisdiction over bankruptcy cases, meaning that these types of cases cannot be heard in state courts.

---

16. The address is http://www.ca4.uscourts.gov.

There are two special trial courts that have nationwide jurisdiction over certain types of cases. First, the Court of International Trade addresses cases involving international trade and customs issues. Second, the United States Court of Federal Claims has jurisdiction over most claims for money damages against the United States, disputes over federal contracts, unlawful "takings" of private property by the federal government, and a variety of other claims against the federal government.

West Virginia is divided into two federal court districts: northern and southern. The Northern District of West Virginia has four court locations: Clarksburg, Elkins, Martinsburg, and Wheeling. Information regarding the Northern District courts can be found at the district's website.[17] The Southern District of West Virginia has four court locations: Beckley, Bluefield, Charleston, and Huntington. Information regarding the Southern District courts can be found at the district's website.[18]

5. Federal Courts Operating Outside the Judicial Branch

Some federal courts and adjudicative bodies are not part of the judicial branch. About 1,400 administrative law judges serve in executive branch departments. These judges conduct hearings, issue or recommend decisions, and enforce agency regulations. Administrative law judges do not receive the federal Constitution's Article III protections. Most of the federal courts operating outside of the judicial branch were established by the Congress to carry out a specific legislative power, such as the determination of taxes or the governance of the armed forces.

III. Finding Cases

A. Digests

1. Overview

Digests are specialized legal research tools that contain case summaries organized by legal topic. West publishes the most popular digests, and they are increasingly being consulted online rather than in the traditional thick print volumes. Unlike case reporters, which organize cases chronologically, West

---

17. The address is http://www.wvnd.uscourts.gov.
18. The address is http://www.wvsd.uscourts.gov.

digests use a "headnote and key number" classification system to organize and summarize cases by subject. This extensive taxonomy saves time, as it allows you to quickly find similar cases on the legal issue under consideration. While digests were once a staple of legal research, modern law students are not as likely to use them, as the artificial intelligence embedded in WestlawNext and Lexis Advance searches often completes the same function of uncovering similar cases on your legal question. However, digest searching can help you get to a very specific point of law more quickly than a broad WestlawNext or Lexis Advance search might.

To help familiarize you with the digest system, Figure 5-2 displays an example of a typical page from the *Virginia and West Virginia Digest*.

Table 5-3 provides a summary of digests that would be particularly helpful for a West Virginia researcher.

As print subscriptions decline, most lawyers who use digests find them on WestlawNext. The system offers searching by headnote and key number, thus allowing you to create your own "custom digest" online.

The West digest system divides the law into more than 400 broad topics and thousands of sub-topics, which are represented by key numbers. For West Virginia researchers, the *Virginia and West Virginia Digest* can be a valuable case-finding tool. The digest contains headnotes for all West Virginia state and federal court decisions from 1681 to date.

2. Introduction to Headnotes and Key Numbers

Before a case is published in a reporter, a West editor reads the case and selects the important issues of law. For each major issue, the editor typically writes a paragraph-long description called a headnote. These headnotes are found at the beginning of each opinion and help the reader to quickly determine the legal issues discussed in the case. While headnotes should not be quoted, they provide an efficient shortcut for finding similar cases.

When writing headnotes, West editors assign each one a topic or "headline," which is actually a broad topic selected from West's list of about 400 possibilities. Examples include "Landlord and Tenant," "Intoxicating Liquors," or "Automobiles." Next, the editor chooses a specific sub-topic, such as "Injury to tenant or occupant." In West digests, this sub-topic is represented by a tiny picture of a key followed by a number, which is known as a key number.

Figure 5-2. Screenshot of the *Virginia and West Virginia Digest*

5E Va D—33

COURTS ☞40.1

For reference to other topics, see Descriptive-Word Index

I. NATURE, EXTENT, AND EXERCISE OF JURISDICTION IN GENERAL.

—Cont'd

(B) LOCATION OF FORUM; FORUM NON CONVENIENS.

☞**40.1. In general.**

W.Va. 2010. Forum non conveniens statute provides guidance to the court in determining what factors weigh more heavily in the determination of whether a case should be heard in an alternate forum. West's Ann.W.Va.Code, 56–1–1(a).
Nezan v. Aries Technologies, Inc., 704 S.E.2d 631, 226 W.Va. 631.

Statutory forum non conveniens provides a mechanism for the court to weigh the various factors, and places emphasis on the plaintiff's choice of forum. West's Ann.W.Va.Code, 56–1–1(a).
Nezan v. Aries Technologies, Inc., 704 S.E.2d 631, 226 W.Va. 631.

W.Va. 1995. Acceptable definition of doctrine of forum non conveniens is that it is nothing more or less than supervening venue provision, permitting displacement of ordinary rules of venue when, in light of certain conditions, trial court thinks that jurisdiction ought to be declined; venue is matter that goes to process rather than substantive rights, i.e., determining which among various competent courts will decide case.
State ex rel. Riffle v. Ranson, 464 S.E.2d 763, 195 W.Va. 121.

W.Va. 1994. Common law doctrine of forum non conveniens is available to courts of record.
Cannelton Industries, Inc. v. Aetna Cas. & Sur. Co. of America, 460 S.E.2d 1, 194 W.Va. 186.

Doctrine of forum non conveniens is applied flexibly to each case.
Cannelton Industries, Inc. v. Aetna Cas. & Sur. Co. of America, 460 S.E.2d 1, 194 W.Va. 186.

Service of suit clause in liability policy, stating that insurer will submit to jurisdiction of any court at insured's request and that "all matters arising hereunder shall be determined in accordance with the law and practice of such Court," allows for court to make determination in accordance with doctrine of forum non

conveniens, if doctrine is available to court.
Cannelton Industries, Inc. v. Aetna Cas. & Sur. Co. of America, 460 S.E.2d 1, 194 W.Va. 186.

W.Va. 1994. Common law doctrine of forum non conveniens is simply that court may, in its own discretion, decline to exercise jurisdiction to promote convenience of witnesses and ends of justice, even when jurisdiction and venue are authorized by letter of statute.
Abbott v. Owens-Corning Fiberglas Corp., 444 S.E.2d 285, 191 W.Va. 198.

Framework to analyze whether common law doctrine of forum non conveniens is applicable is that set forth in Supreme Court of Appeals' *Norfolk and Western Ry. Co. v. Tsapis* decision; this framework ensures that doctrine of forum non conveniens is applied flexibly and on case-by-case basis.
Abbott v. Owens-Corning Fiberglas Corp., 444 S.E.2d 285, 191 W.Va. 198.

Doctrine of forum non conveniens is drastic remedy which should be used with caution and restraint.
Abbott v. Owens-Corning Fiberglas Corp., 444 S.E.2d 285, 191 W.Va. 198.

W.Va. 1993. State courts are free to apply forum non conveniens doctrine in FELA cases, when appropriate, as FELA does not require state courts to entertain suits arising under it. Federal Employers' Liability Act, § 6, 45 U.S.C.A. § 56.
Norfolk Southern Ry. Co. v. Maynard, 437 S.E.2d 277, 190 W.Va. 113.

W.Va. 1990. Doctrine of forum non conveniens could be applied to case brought under Federal Employers' Liability Act (FELA). Federal Employers' Liability Act, §§ 1–10, as amended, 45 U.S.C.A. §§ 51–60.
Norfolk and Western Ry. Co. v. Tsapis, 400 S.E.2d 239, 184 W.Va. 231.

Common-law principle of forum non conveniens is applicable only if, as threshold matter, forum court has jurisdiction and venue is proper under statute.
Norfolk and Western Ry. Co. v. Tsapis, 400 S.E.2d 239, 184 W.Va. 231.

† This Case was not selected for publication in the National Reporter System

Source: Reprinted with permission of West.

As an example, Figure 5-3 provides a screenshot of the third headnote in the landmark U.S. Supreme Court *Gideon v. Wainwright*[19] opinion. This particular headnote describes one major issue in the case: whether an indigent defendant in a criminal prosecution in state court has the right to appointed counsel. West editors categorized the broad topic of the headnote as "Constitutional Law" and assigned the key number of 4809, which represents the subtopic of "Counsel, Appointment of Counsel."

The beauty of the West digest system lies in its consistency across jurisdictions; key numbers are the same in all West digests for all jurisdictions. Therefore, once you have located the topic and key number for the point of law at issue in your case, it is easy to find that point of law across jurisdictional boundaries. For example, to find West Virginia cases on the same topic as the Supreme Court case above, you would use the same topic (Constitutional Law), combine it with the key number 4809, and then open the corresponding *Virginia and West Virginia Digest.*

Figure 5-3. West Headnote Example

2	Constitutional Law	92	Constitutional Law	
	Where provision of	92XXVII	Due Process	ntial to fair trial, it is made obligatory on
	states by Fourteenth	92XXVII(H)	Criminal Law	
		92XXVII(H)10	Counsel	
	880 Cases that cite	92k4809	Appointment of counsel	
			(Formerly 92k268.2(3))	

3 Constitutional Law 🗝 Appointment of counsel

Sixth Amendment to federal Constitution providing that in all criminal prosecutions the accused shall enjoy right to assistance of counsel for his defense is made obligatory on the states by the Fourteenth Amendment, and indigent defendant in criminal prosecution in state court has right to have counsel appointed for him. Betts v. Brady, 316 U.S. 455, 62 S.Ct. 1252, overruled. U.S.C.A.Const. Amends. 6, 14.

4420 Cases that cite this headnote

Source: Reprinted with permission of West.

3. Step-by-Step Guide to Using Digests

a. Step One: Isolate a Topic and Key Number

To begin your exploration of the digest system, start by targeting one or more topics and key numbers of interest. There are several ways to identify useful topics and key numbers. If you already have a good case on your topic, simply look at the headnote for the issue you are researching to isolate the appropriate topic and key number.

---

19. *Gideon v. Wainwright,* 372 U.S. 335 (1963).

Table 5-3. Digests Helpful to a West Virginia Researcher

Digest	Coverage
Virginia and West Virginia Digest	West Virginia Cases
South Eastern Digest	Cases from *South Eastern Reporter**
Decennial Digest	Cases from all West reporters
Federal Practice Digest	Cases from Federal District Courts, Appellate Courts, and U.S. Supreme Court
United States Supreme Court Digest	Cases from U.S. Supreme Court

* The *South Eastern Reporter* covers opinions and decisions from 1939 to date issued by the state courts of Georgia, North Carolina, South Carolina, Virginia and West Virginia.

If you have not already identified a good case with headnotes to launch your research, there are numerous methods for beginning. Many of the secondary sources and finding tools discussed in Chapter 2 would provide an effective start, including encyclopedias, law reviews, and the annotated codes discussed in Chapter 4. Once you have identified a relevant case, find the headnote that provides the point of law you need.

b. Step Two: Select the Appropriate Digest
The second step is usually straightforward: choose the best digest for your needs. Table 5-4 lists major digests that regularly provide assistance to West Virginia researchers.

Table 5-4. Major Digests for West Virginia Researchers

Digest Name	Description of Contents
West's Virginia and West Virginia Digest	This Digest contains headnotes, classified according to West's® Key Number System, for all Virginia and West Virginia state and federal court decisions dating from 1681 to the present. Each volume is supplemented by a pocket part and the full set is also supplemented by interim pamphlets.
South Eastern Digest	This Digest contains headnotes for Georgia, North Carolina, South Carolina, Virginia, and West Virginia court decisions issued from 1934 to the present. Each volume is supplemented by a pocket part and the full set is also supplemented by interim pamphlets.

c. Step Three: Read Headnotes and Pull Cases

The last step is also straightforward, but sometimes more time consuming. Find your digest, select the volume containing your topic, locate your key number, and read the headnotes listed under it to find useful cases. If you are completing this process online, simply retrieve headnotes with your key numbers on Westlaw. It is important never to cite a case directly from the digest, as the headnote contains only limited information about the case. Instead, note the citations of interest, and then use the citations to find the cases that you want to read. Read the opinions and then decide whether they merit inclusion in your document.

B. Citators

1. Introduction

Lawyers need to rely on current, valid authorities—using "bad law," meaning law that is no longer valid because it has been overruled or superseded, is the equivalent of a Major League Baseball player dropping an easy pop fly. Thankfully, citator services provide a relatively painless way to avoid this rookie error.

When lawyers talk about citators, they are referring to specialized tools that help them determine two things: (1) whether an authority is still "good law," and (2) which other sources have cited that authority. While the first use is the most widely known as a required step in thorough legal research, smart researchers use citators to create a list of additional sources on the same topic.

For example, imagine that you have located an on-point case for the topic you've been asked to research. By entering that case citation into a citator tool, you will receive a list of all sources that have cited that case. You can see why a researcher would want to check out those cases, and then use them to flesh out the sections of a memo or brief where controlling rules are discussed.

Lexis, Westlaw, and Bloomberg Law all offer electronic citator services. (Most libraries no longer carry print citators, as the electronic options are far superior to the cumbersome and difficult-to-navigate print volumes.) The process is similar no matter which citator you use, but the tools go by different names: Shepard's on Lexis, KeyCite on Westlaw, and BCite on Bloomberg Law.

Because Shepard's was the most well-known citator for many years, many lawyers say "Shepardize" to refer to the process of checking to make sure a case is still good law. It doesn't matter which citator you use to determine the status of the case, even if you are instructed to "Shepardize." Further, remember that citators are not just for cases; you can "Shepardize" any authority, from a statute to a law review article.

2. Using Citators to Assess the Validity of Legal Authorities[20]

Legal researchers are held to high ethical standards; it is crucial to validate every case and make sure the points of law in the case have not been overruled before you rely on them. When you enter a case citation into a citator tool, the service will generate a report that shows every authority in which that case has been referenced, all treatments of the case, and, sometimes most importantly, whether or not the case remains "good law."

The reports generated by citator services generally include the following: (1) case name, citation, court designation, and year; (2) prior case history and subsequent appellate history; and (3) editorial "enhancements" that caution the researcher about possible negative treatment, such as a yellow triangle or a red flag. Cases flagged for negative treatment warrant careful review, as they indicate that your authority may have been criticized or even overruled by later decisions.

The editorial icons are similar across systems. Generally, a red-colored symbol (flag or stop sign) means that the case has undergone negative treatment and might have been overruled, so proceed with caution. Red-colored treatments do not necessarily preclude the use of a case, as it may have been overruled on other grounds (for reasons other than your point of law) or on a different point of law altogether, but proceed carefully. If possible, try to find a case where you won't need to explain why the red signal does not apply. Figure 5-4 features a KeyCite report with negative history.

Yellow-colored treatments mean that there is some negative history, but parts of the case remain good law. The case has not been reversed or overruled, but perhaps the reasoning of the decision has been criticized or the holding limited to a specific set of facts. Responsible researchers investigate the reason for the yellow sign and then determine whether the case is usable.

Green-colored signals mean that courts have treated the case positively, so there should not be a problem citing to it. Figure 5-5 shows an example of a case that has received positive treatment, and therefore is still good law, via the Shepard's citator system.

---

20. Citators can be used to validate most legal authorities—not just cases. Always use a citator before including an authority in a legal memorandum or brief.

Figure 5-4. WestlawNext KeyCite Report with Negative History

KeyCite. **Minersville School Dist. v. Gobitis**
Supreme Court of the United States.   June 3, 1940   310 U.S. 586   60 S.Ct. 1010   (Approx. 11 pages)

Document   Filings (4)   Negative Treatment (10)   History (4)   Citing References (1,489)   Powered by KeyCite

Negative Treatment

☐ Select all items   No items selected

Negative Direct History
The KeyCited document has been negatively impacted in the following ways by events or decisions in the same litigation or proceedings:

There is no negative direct history.

Negative Citing References (10)
The KeyCited document has been negatively referenced by the following events or decisions in other litigation or proceedings:

	Treatment	Title	Date	Type	Depth	Headnote(s)
☐	Overruled by	1. West Virginia State Board of Education v. Barnette ⟫ MOST NEGATIVE 319 U.S. 624, U.S.W.Va. Suit by Walter Barnette and others against the West Virginia State Board of Education, etc., and others for an injunction to restrain enforcement of a regulation requiring children....	Jun. 14 , 1943	Case	▮▮▮▮	8 9 10 S.Ct.
☐	Overruling Recognized by	2. Employment Div., Dept. of Human Resources of Oregon v. Smith ⟫ 494 U.S. 872, U.S.Or. Claimants sought review of determination that their religious use of peyote, which resulted in their dismissal from employment, was "misconduct" disqualifying them from receipt...	Apr. 17 , 1990	Case	▮▮▮▮	7 8 S.Ct.

Source: Reprinted with permission of West.

Figure 5-5. Lexis Advance Shepard's Report with Positive History

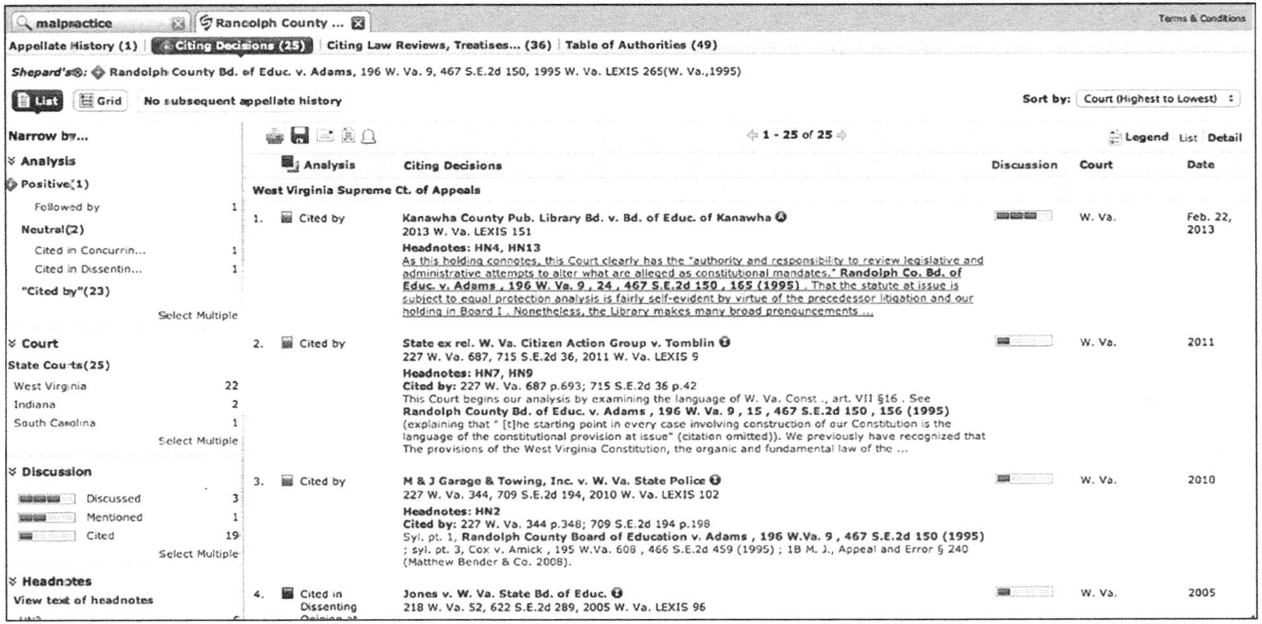

Source: Reprinted with permission of LexisNexis.

All citator systems allow you to focus on negative treatment to quickly determine whether the authority in question should be used.

In January 2017, Lexis introduced a new feature called "Reasons for Shepard's Signal," which makes it easier to quickly leap from your full-text case to the passage that was editorially selected as having the strongest influence on the Shepard's signal. While the service initially applied to cases marked with a Warning (stop sign) or Caution (triangle) treatment from 2003 and beyond, Lexis plans to expand the service to include both earlier cases as well as those marked with the "questioned" treatment.

3. Using Citators to Find Cases

Many researchers overlook the citator as a means of finding additional cases, but this is a mistake. As soon as you have located any relevant primary authority, enter it into a citator to receive a list of cases that have cited to your entry. Then, review those cases; the cases that are cited frequently in subsequent case law probably merit review and possible inclusion in your memo or brief.

C. Finding Case Law Via Online Searching

1. Lexis and Westlaw

With Lexis Advance and WestlawNext offering Google-like searches, finding cases via these subscription services is easier than ever. Both offer a search box at the top of the page where researchers can enter citations, case names, or search terms. Detailed guides for using these products are available on the Lexis Advance and WestlawNext websites. Be sure to adjust the jurisdiction-limiting tab near the search bar to narrow your case law search to your desired locale.

All cases published in West reporters (as well as many unpublished cases) can be retrieved on Lexis and Westlaw. Cases typically appear within hours of their release by the courts. A published case retrieved on either system includes editorial enhancements, such as the synopsis and headnotes.

2. Fastcase

Members of the West Virginia State Bar receive a free membership to Fastcase, a legal research service that includes primary law from all 50 states and deep federal coverage. Almost all published West Virginia cases are available through Fastcase. The collection includes cases, statutes, regulations, court rules, and constitutions, as well as access to a newspaper archive, legal forms, and a PACER[21] search of federal filings. While the citator service on Fastcase cannot compete with the commercial citators, researchers can rely on Fastcase for many basic research needs.

3. PACER for Federal Cases and Filings

Public Access to Court Electronic Records (PACER) is an electronic public access service that allows researchers to electronically obtain case and docket information from federal courts and the PACER Case Locator. While PACER provides access to federal judicial opinions and case filings, it is not as useful as the commercial services for finding cases by citation. PACER searching is easiest if you know the deciding court and docket number for the case. For instance, consider the following example:

Ohio Valley Environmental Coalition, Inc. v. Fola Coal Company, LLC, 82 F.Supp.3d 673 (S.D. W. Va. 2015)

While this citation is easy to locate via commercial databases, to find it on PACER, you would need both the case citation and docket number to retrieve the case without executing an advanced search. Thus, it is often much easier to use a commercial source or even a free source to retrieve cases. However, PACER provides access to not only the desired judicial opinion but also to all public filings in the case. Bloomberg Law offers comprehensive coverage of documents available on PACER, and Westlaw and Lexis continue to add coverage of court filings.

4. Google Scholar

Researchers are increasingly turning to Google Scholar as a source for accessing both state and federal judicial opinions. While a typical Google search would yield documents and websites where a case citation appears, Google Scholar will retrieve the judicial opinion itself—for free! Citations to other cases that can be accessed via Google Scholar will be hyperlinked in the opinion. While this resource does not provide the editorial enhancements available through paid sites, it is a cost-effective way to find cases and other basic information about how a case has been cited.

---

21. PACER is the acronym for Public Access to Court Electronic Records, the federal judiciary's electronic public access service. It allows you to obtain case and docket information from federal appellate, district and bankruptcy courts for free via the Internet. The address is www.pacer.gov. Bloomberg Law also provides access to PACER.

Table 5-5. Step-by-Step Guide to Finding Cases

Step 1: Use one of more of the following entry points to assemble a list of citations to potentially relevant cases • Secondary source like Michie's Jurisprudence • Annotated code like Michie's Code • Westlaw Next or Lexis Advance search • Google search
Step 2: Pare down your list of potentially relevant cases to a list of promising cases by skimming the headnotes of those cases and locating the best of the bunch.
Step 3: Expand your possibilities by reading cases cited by a leading case and by using a citator to generate more leads.
Step 4: Carefully analyze your leading possibilities and determine whether you should pursue additional search terms or lines of cases.
Step 5: If you believe you need to pursue a new path, do that now.
Step 6: Use a citator to validate every case that you are considering for your memorandum or brief.

5. Internet Research

A variety of websites can provide researchers with case law; these options are discussed in depth in Chapter 9.

Table 5-5 summarizes the various paths you can take to assemble a list of leads to potentially relevant cases.

IV. Citing Cases

Details for citing case law are provided in Chapter 10, but here are two examples (one state case, one federal case) for quick reference:

- West Virginia: *Bruceton Bank v. U.S. Fid. and Guar. Ins. Co.*, 486 S.E.2d 19 (W. Va. 1997)

- Federal: *Cmty. Bank & Trust Co. v. Copses*, 953 F.2d 133 (4th Cir. 1991)

V. Additional Resources

Lexis Advance Guides
> http://help.lexisnexis.com/tabula-rasa/newlexis/home?lbu=US&locale=
> en_US&audience=all,res,shep,lpa,lps,med,pub,vsa

Northern District of West Virginia
> http://www.wvnd.uscourts.gov

Southern District of West Virginia
> http://www.wvsd.uscourts.gov

United States Court of Appeals for the Fourth Circuit
> http://www.ca4.uscourts.gov

United States Supreme Court
> http://www.supremecourt.gov

West Virginia Supreme Court
> http://www.courtswv.gov/supreme-court/index.html

WestlawNext Guides
> http://legalsolutions.thomsonreuters.com/law-products/product-support/
> user-guides

Chapter Six

Researching Administrative Law

I. Introduction to Administrative Law

For newer lawyers who tend to feel more comfortable with case law and statutory rules, it may come as a surprise that many West Virginia lawyers spend their careers immersed in a different sort of legal authority—state agency regulations. Lawyers must deal with a bounty of state and federal regulations, which provide the details on how to comply with statutory law. In essence, while statutes broadly explain what the legislature intends the law to be, regulations get down to the nitty gritty, spelling out exactly how to comply.

Administrative law refers to the body of law surrounding governmental agencies. These agencies develop expertise in particular areas (e.g., environmental safety, alcoholic beverage control, revenue collection) and then promulgate rules accordingly. (Note: The terms "rules" and "regulations" are used interchangeably in administrative law.) In essence, administrative agencies perform functions of all three branches of government—a legislative function through rulemaking, a judicial function through administrative law hearings, and an executive function through enforcement of regulations by agency personnel. Because so much activity takes place in the administrative arena, you should remain on the lookout for records of agency activity in all three realms.

Though agencies carry out laws enacted by the legislative branch, most are connected with the executive branch of government. Agencies find their power in enabling statutes passed by the Legislature. These special laws define the scope of a particular agency's authority and outline the contours of the agency's power. For example, the Legislature may grant an agency the power to settle disputes via specialized administrative courts. While those decisions may only bind the parties involved, they can be useful to researchers who are trying to predict future decision-making.

The Administrative Law Division of the West Virginia Secretary of State's Office serves as the state's official clearinghouse for agency rules, notices, orders, decisions, and other procedural documents. Through online information, subscriptions, and extensive imaged historical files, the division provides public access to the requirements and procedures of West Virginia state agencies and boards. You can even take questions straight to the division by telephone at (304) 558-6000 or via e-mail at adlaw@wvsos.com.

II. Administrative Law and Governmental Agencies in West Virginia

Administrative law plays a key role in the lives of many West Virginia lawyers—with more than 210 agencies in the state, some practitioners spend the bulk of their time navigating agency rules. You should consider administrative regulations to be a form of primary authority, even though West Virginia publishes them in loose-leaf binders instead of more formal, hardbound books. In addition, executive orders of the Governor and attorney general opinions fall under the administrative law umbrella and can be useful to legal researchers.

Chapter 29A of the West Virginia Code contains the Administrative Procedures Act, which defines the scope of agency power within the state. The Act defines agencies as "any state board, commission, department, office or officer authorized by law to make rules or adjudicate contested cases, except those in the legislative or judicial branches."[1] The Legislative Rule Making Review Committee and the Administrative Law Division of the Secretary of State are responsible for administering the Act.

A comprehensive list of West Virginia state agencies with website links is available on the West Virginia State government website.[2]

A. Administrative Rules and Rulemaking in West Virginia

1. Rulemaking through the Standard Process

Agencies develop policy through rulemaking, and as such, legal researchers must be careful to analyze relevant agency regulations in their memoranda and briefs. Three primary types of rules populate West Virginia state admin-

---

1. W. Va. Code Ann. § 29A-1-2(a) (West 2017).
2. The address is http://www.wv.gov/agencies/Pages/default.aspx.

istrative law: legislative rules, procedural rules, and interpretive rules. Legislative rules are the only type under the Administrative Procedures Act that carry the force of law; they can supply a basis for civil or criminal liability, or grant or deny a specific benefit. Legislative rules do not include findings of fact made by an agency, declaratory rulings issued by an agency, orders, or executive orders by the Governor. Legislative rules are proposed by an agency, but must be approved by the West Virginia Legislature before they go into effect, unless they are labeled as emergency rules.

All proposed legislative rules, except emergency rules, are submitted to a joint committee of the Legislature called the Legislative Rule Making Review Committee. The committee reviews all proposed legislative rules and may hold public hearings. In its rulemaking capacity, the committee must consider the following: whether the agency has exceeded its authority in proposing the approved rule, whether the proposed rule conforms with legislative intent, whether the proposed rule conflicts with other provisions of the West Virginia Code or agency rules, whether the proposed rule is reasonable and necessary to accomplish its stated objectives, whether the proposed rule is easily understandable, and whether the proposed rule complies with the Administrative Procedures Act.

The Committee then makes a recommendation to the Legislature; it can recommend that the agency be authorized to promulgate the rule before it is finalized, or it can suggest amendments to or a complete withdrawal of the rule.

The other types of administrative rules — procedural and interpretive — are not reviewed by the Legislature. Procedural rules determine rules of practice, procedure, or evidence for hearings before agencies and can include forms. Interpretive rules provide guidance on the agency's interpretations, policies, or opinions, but may not be used to determine issues affected by private rights.

Before procedural or interpretative rules may be promulgated, an agency must provide public notice. To do so, an agency must file the proposed text in the *West Virginia Register* (discussed later in this chapter).

2. Emergency Rules

One other type of rule that can avoid legislative scrutiny is the emergency rule, which may be promulgated only when an emergency exists or when the law specifically authorizes an emergency rule to be implemented before the next legislative session. The West Virginia Code defines emergency narrowly, allowing rules to be promulgated only "(1) for the immediate preservation of the public peace, health, safety or welfare, (2) to comply with a time limitation established by this code or by a federal statute or regulation, or (3) to prevent substantial harm to the public interest."[3]

The steps for promulgating an emergency rule are very specific, and missing a deadline can cause the rule to die, without an easy way for the agency to correct the problem. The steps are quite technical, and it would be prudent to check with an expert (either in the Secretary of State's Office or in your law office) to ensure that the requirements have been satisfied.

Generally, to propose an emergency rule, an agency must file with both the Secretary of State and the Legislative Rule Making Review Committee. The Secretary of State then has 42 days to review the rule and decide if a true emergency exists. (If the Secretary of State files an emergency rule, the Attorney General holds review power.) If an emergency rule is not approved, the agency may still proceed through the standard rulemaking process.

B. Contested Administrative Law Cases in West Virginia

West Virginia law requires that parties be given an opportunity to be heard in proceedings "before an agency in which the legal rights, duties, interests or privileges of specific parties are required by law or constitutional right to be determined after an agency hearing."[4] Cases in which an agency "issues a license, permit or certificate after an examination" are specifically excluded.[5] Written notice is required at least ten days before a hearing occurs.[6]

Each agency adopts rules of procedure for hearing contested cases.[7] Some agencies have authority to issue subpoenas and may seek enforcement of those subpoenas in circuit court.

The West Virginia Code requires impartial hearings in contested cases;[8] either the West Virginia Rules of Evidence or more detailed evidentiary rules discussed in agency regulations apply. All parties have the right to cross-examine testifying witnesses. Final orders of agency decisions must be in writing and must include findings of fact and conclusions of law.

---

3. W. Va. Code Ann. § 29A-3-15(f) (West 2017).
4. W. Va. Code Ann. § 29A-1-2(b) (West 2017).
5. Id.
6. W. Va. Code Ann. § 29A-5-1(a) (West 2017).
7. See id.
8. W. Va. Code Ann. § 29A-5-1(d) (West 2017).

Final agency orders and decisions are subject to judicial review. To initiate this process, a petitioner may file either in Kanawha County or in the circuit court of the county in which the petitioner resides or does business.[9] The agency and other parties of record must be served with a copy of the petition; the appeal can be based on questions of either law or fact or both. The reviewing court examines the record and may hear oral arguments, which require written briefs.

Any adversely affected party may appeal the final judgment of the circuit court to the West Virginia Supreme Court of Appeals. The scope of judicial review is narrow; the Supreme Court reviews the record to determine if the evidence presented supports the agency's findings.

Generally, where an administrative remedy is provided by statute or regulation, relief must be sought through the respective administrative body initially. The courts may only intervene after this remedy has been exhausted.[10]

III. Researching West Virginia Administrative Law

A. Sources of West Virginia Administrative Rules and Regulations

1. The West Virginia Code of State Rules

a. Introduction to the Code of State Rules

The West Virginia Code of State Rules, commonly referred to as the CSR, is the official compilation of West Virginia's administrative regulations.

The CSR, which contains more than 1,500 regulations, is organized by title, with each title representing a department, commission, board, or agency. CSR titles are further divided into series and sections. Each regulation contains the rule text, a source of statutory authority statement, a filing date, and an effective date.

The West Virginia Secretary of State's office stopped publishing a print version of the CSR in 2013.

Though West Virginia practitioners (and sometimes courts) often cite the CSR as "W. Va. C.S.R.," the *Bluebook* suggests a slightly different abbreviation. To cite to title 114, series 23, section 1.1 of the CSR, standard citation form

---

9. W. Va. Code Ann. § 29A-5-4(b) (West 2017).
10. See W. Va. Code Ann. § 29A-5-4(a) (West 2017).

would be as follows: W. Va. Code R. § 114-23-1.1 (2017). The 2017 date refers to the date listed on the annual Code of State Rules Index, located in the Table of Contents and User's Guide volume of the CSR.

b. Searching for Rules in the CSR

The West Virginia Secretary of State's Office maintains an unofficial version of the Code of State Rules, with search capacity, on its website.[11] From the main page, you can search by agency or title and series; you can also perform a full-text search for a specific word. However, these regulations are typically easier to locate via commercial databases.

c. Updating the CSR

Rules change—and require CSR updates—when government is reorganized, when agency names change, or when the Legislature creates, merges, renames, or terminates boards or commissions. While the changes come in cycles, it is almost impossible to keep track of every detail. As always, ask a librarian or consult the Secretary of State's Office to be sure that the rule you are relying on is current.

If commercial databases are not an option, researchers should check the *West Virginia Register*, which is searchable under the Administrative Law tab of the Secretary of State's website, for any revisions or proposed revisions.[12]

2. The *West Virginia Register*

The *West Virginia Register*,[13] published weekly, contains information about proposed rule changes. A chronological index appears at the start of the publication and lists the proposed rule changes for the week. A list of public hearings, also known as the Open Government Meetings Listing, follows the index and includes the location, date, and purpose of upcoming hearings.

3. Executive Agency Records, Orders, Opinions, and Decisions

The Administrative Law Division of the Secretary of State's Office is the official repository of executive agency orders, opinions, and decisions. When an

---

11. The website is http://apps.sos.wv.gov/adlaw/registers/.

12. If you have access to commercial databases, a citator tool (such as Shepard's or Keycite) will allow you to validate the currency of your regulation without these cumbersome steps.

13. The West Virginia Register may also be referred to as the State Register.

official copy is required for a legal action or other purpose, researchers can make online purchases via the Secretary of State's website.

Orders issued by the Governor are filed both for archival purposes and for notice in the *West Virginia Register* with the Secretary of State.

a. Executive Records

The Secretary of State has served as the keeper of the Governor's official papers since West Virginia became a state. The provisions of the West Virginia Code relating to the general powers and duties of the Governor, Secretary of State, and other officials are derived from the laws of Virginia.

Original signed copies of specific types of formal documents executed by the Governor and countersigned by the Secretary of State are filed with the Secretary's office. In addition, the executive records section serves as repository for other legal documents, often as a result of specific legislation.

The executive records section maintains two broad categories of records: *Executive Journal* records and miscellaneous records. In the bound volumes of the *Executive Journal* records, researchers will find documents reflecting official acts of the governor. The Secretary of State has been assigned as the keeper of various other miscellaneous records, either by a constitutional provision or by statute. Although these are not the Governor's papers, they are maintained by the executive records section. All information is public and available for inspection and copying.

b. Attorney General Opinions

Most often, advice of the Attorney General is provided to agencies and is not considered to be an official opinion. However, when an official opinion is issued, it is filed for publication in the *West Virginia Register*. Official opinions are not considered to have the same force of law as a court opinion, but weight is given to these opinions when other official interpretations are lacking. The Attorney General may also give advice to state agencies concerning everyday operations. The Attorney General's website provides details.[14]

c. Ethics Opinions

The West Virginia Ethics Commission was created by the Legislature in 1989 to implement a code of conduct for public officials. The Commission issues official advisory opinions on matters of ethical conduct and on the application of the Ethics Act and the Open Governmental Meetings Act. These

---

14. The web address is https://ago.wv.gov/Pages/default.aspx.

opinions, available on the Ethics Commission website, also address the Administrative Law Judge Code of Conduct and the actions of county school boards.[15]

d. Grievance Decisions

The West Virginia Grievance Board was created in 1985 to resolve employment problems and disputes between employees and county boards of education, higher education institutions, and state agencies. The board conducts hearings on grievances and issues official opinions. Official copies are available from the Secretary of State, and the text of the opinions can be accessed online at the Grievance Board website.[16]

IV. Federal Administrative Law

A. Introduction

Federal administrative law is a subject worthy of its own book, but the primary resources used by legal researchers in this area are considered below. You should be aware that federal regulations are complicated and, if you are delving deeply into them, you will want to find additional training opportunities and more detailed instruction.

Federal administrative law mirrors state administrative law, but the copious regulations fill even more library shelves. The process for finding and understanding federal administrative rules and regulations, however, is quite similar.

B. The Code of Federal Regulations

Just as West Virginia codifies its agency regulations in the CSR, federal administrative law is codified in the Code of Federal Regulations. (The Code of Federal Regulations is commonly referred to as the "CFR.") Published by the Office of the Federal Register, an agency of the National Archives and Records Administration, the CFR's fifty titles fill more than 200 volumes. Each title represents a broad area of law that is subject to federal regulation.

The final rules promulgated by federal agencies and published in the *Federal Register* are ultimately reorganized by topic or subject matter and codified in the Code of Federal Regulations, which receives an annual update.

---

15. The web address is http://ethics.wv.gov/Pages/default.aspx.
16. The web address is http://pegb.wv.gov/Pages/default.aspx.

And just as every West Virginia regulation must have a source of statutory authority, every CFR regulation must have a corresponding enabling statute. The rationale for delegating power to agencies is the same in the federal context. Congress is often too busy or gridlocked to write statutes that cover the minutiae required in regulatory matters. It often makes sense to delegate rulemaking authority to technical specialists who should be better equipped to draft these regulations. As such, under the federal Administrative Procedure Act, federal agencies are allowed to promulgate rules and regulations through a public rule-making process.

On its Electronic Code of Federal Regulations (e-CFR) website, the Government Printing Office provides free access to an unofficial version of the CFR that is generally just a few days behind real time. You can browse broadly, limit your search to a particular field or CFR title, or use "Boolean" or proximity searches if you have terms to insert.

C. The *Federal Register*

The *Federal Register* is the official daily journal of the United States government (similar to the *West Virginia Register*). It contains proposed new rules and regulations of federal agencies, final rules, changes to existing rules, and notices of meeting and adjudicatory proceedings.

The *Federal Register* is compiled by the Office of the Federal Register (housed within the National Archives and Records Administration); the Government Printing Office prints the official version. Of course, the commercial databases provide unofficial versions.

D. Decisions of Federal Administrative Agencies

Because administrative agencies have quasi-judicial functions, they conduct hearings and issue decisions through administrative law judges. These opinions can be difficult to locate, as there is no single database containing every opinion. The procedures and publications of federal agency activities vary widely.

About fifteen agencies currently publish decisions in court reporter form. Like federal rules and regulations, these agency decisions are available in several different places: officially published reports of decisions, commercial databases, agency websites, and via loose-leaf services. Because of the fragmented nature of these publications, always check with a librarian if your research requires a review of federal administrative agency opinions.

Some official agency publications, such as the Federal Trade Commission Decisions, resemble typical court reporters. Table 1.2 of *The Bluebook: A Uni-*

form System of Citation lists many official and commercial publications covering administrative adjudications, interpretations, and opinions of the major federal regulatory agencies. Administrative decisions are also available on Lexis, Westlaw, and Bloomberg Law.

V. Citing Administrative Regulations

Details for citing to administrative rules and regulations appear in Chapter 10, but for quick reference, here are some examples:

- West Virginia: W. Va. Code R. §61-8-3 (2017)
- Federal: 7 C.F.R. §33.50 (2018)

VI. Additional Resources

Code of Federal Regulations
    http://www.gpo.gov/fdsys/browse/collectionCfr.action?collectionCode=
    CFR

Comprehensive List of West Virginia State Agencies
    http://www.wv.gov/agencies/Pages/default.aspx

Cornell's Wex Dictionary on Administrative Law
    http://www.law.cornell.edu/wex/administrative_law

Federal Register
    https://www.federalregister.gov

West Virginia Attorney General
    https://ago.wv.gov/Pages/default.aspx

West Virginia Code of State Rules
    http://apps.sos.wv.gov/adlaw/csr

West Virginia Ethics Commission
    http://www.ethics.wv.gov/Pages/default.aspx

West Virginia Executive Records
    http://www.sos.wv.gov/public-services/execrecords/Pages/Executive
    RecordsServices.aspx

West Virginia Grievance Board
    http://pegb.wv.gov/Pages/default.aspx

West Virginia Register
    http://www.sos.wv.gov/administrative-law/register/Pages/default.aspx

West Virginia Secretary of State
  http://www.sos.wv.gov

Chapter Seven

Rules of Court and Ethics

I. Introduction to Court Rules

It is hard to overstate the importance of court rules. In addition to the Rules of Civil Procedure, Rules of Appellate Procedure, Rules of Criminal Procedure, and Rules of Evidence that most law students are familiar with, individual courts establish supplemental rules that lawyers often refer to generically as "local rules." A researcher who ignores local rules can wind up missing a deadline that he didn't know existed—but would have easily satisfied had he checked this specialized source of authority. Local court rules often provide more specific requirements than the broad rules listed above, so researchers must consult these additional rules frequently.

For example, detailed rules on electronic filing and motions to disqualify a judge are contained in the West Virginia Trial Court Rules—not the more general West Virginia Rules of Civil Procedure. After you determine the jurisdiction in which you will be filing, review these specialized rules carefully, as they often provide practical requirements not contained elsewhere.

West Virginia court rules are available on the West Virginia Judiciary's website and also at the end of the print volumes of the West Virginia Code, which are discussed in depth in Chapter 4.

II. West Virginia Court Rules

West Virginia practitioners are subject to numerous sets of court rules. The highlights are provided below.

A. Supreme Court Proceedings

The Rules of Appellate Procedure "govern procedure: (1) in appeals and certified questions from lower courts and other tribunals to the Supreme Court of Appeals of West Virginia; (2) in proceedings in the Supreme Court of Appeals for review of orders of administrative agencies, boards, commissions, and officers of the State of West Virginia; and (3) in applications for writs or other relief, over which the Supreme Court of Appeals has jurisdiction."[1] This set of rules addresses matters such as the requirements for properly filing an appeal, the record on appeal, and the form and filing of appellate documents.

B. Circuit Court Proceedings

Proceedings in Circuit Courts (West Virginia's trial courts) are governed by multiple sets of rules that arise during different stages of the litigation process—or that may not arise at all because of the type of litigation. For instance, the Rules of Criminal Procedure do not apply in civil action suits. The various rules governing trial court proceedings, discussed next, should be consulted well before filing a brief or entering the courtroom.

1. Rules of Civil Procedure

The Rules of Civil Procedure govern the procedure for all civil actions, suits, or other judicial proceedings in West Virginia circuit courts. They are to be "construed and administered to secure the just, speedy, and inexpensive determination of every action."[2] The Rules of Civil Procedure address matters such as the form of pleadings and motions, which parties may be joined to a proceeding, the scope and limits of discovery, the selection of jurors, and the entry of judgment.

---

1. W. Va. R. App. P. 1(a).
2. W. Va. R. Civ. P. 1.

2. Rules of Criminal Procedure

The Rules of Criminal Procedure govern the procedure for all criminal actions in West Virginia circuit courts. Some of the rules specify that they also apply to criminal proceedings in West Virginia magistrate courts. These rules address matters such as search and seizure, indictment proceedings, pleas, venue, sentencing, and appeals.

3. Rules of Evidence

The Rules of Evidence apply, with certain exceptions,[3] to all proceedings in the courts of West Virginia. The rules govern the presentation of evidence in court. For example, these rules address issues such as whether evidence is authenticated, whether character evidence is admissible, whether evidence is relevant, which evidence may be used for purposes of impeachment, and whether expert testimony is admissible.

4. Trial Court Rules

The Trial Court Rules refer to a body of rules that relate to court administration in civil and criminal matters. These rules apply to all West Virginia circuit courts and are intended to supersede earlier local rules that varied by circuit. The Trial Court Rules also cover topics such as the procedure for filing a motion to disqualify a judge, electronic filing, and mass litigation.

5. Rules Governing Post-Conviction Habeas Corpus Proceedings

These rules provide the procedure for post-conviction habeas corpus proceedings, which are filed to attack a conviction or sentence on constitutional grounds. They supplement the procedures set forth in the West Virginia Code.[4] The rules address the filing of petitions, appointment of counsel, discovery, and evidentiary hearings as they relate to post-conviction habeas corpus proceedings.

6. Rules of Procedure for Administrative Appeals

This set of rules governs circuit court procedure for judicial review of final orders or decisions from agencies, including contested cases that are governed

---

3. WVRE 1101.
4. W. Va. Code Ann. § 53-4A-11 (LexisNexis 2017).

by the West Virginia Administrative Procedures Act. These Rules address commencement of an appeal, proper form for briefs, and the stay of decisions pending appeal.

7. Rules of Practice and Procedure for Minor Guardianship Proceedings

Circuit court and family court minor guardianship proceedings are governed by a special set of rules. Minor guardianship is a legal arrangement giving someone the authority to make decisions on a minor's behalf. If this set of rules conflicts with other rules or statutes, these specialized rules trump. Some matters addressed by these rules include the elements of a petition for appointing a guardian, the nomination and screening of guardians, and confidentiality.

8. Rules of Practice and Procedure for Domestic Violence Civil Proceedings

A special set of rules applies to domestic violence proceedings, whether they are held in West Virginia circuit courts, family courts, or magistrate courts. If this set of rules conflicts with other rules or statutes, these specialized rules trump. These rules address many of the family law issues surrounding domestic violence causes of action. Specifically, these rules address the waiver of fees for indigents, the consolidation of multiple cases involving the same parties, emergency protective orders, and child protective investigations.

9. Rules of Procedure for Child Abuse and Neglect Proceedings

The Rules of Procedure for Child Abuse and Neglect Proceedings govern the procedural aspects of child abuse proceedings. If a conflict arises, these rules trump other West Virginia rules and statutes. Some of the matters addressed by these rules include emergency custody, foster care review, and status conferences with the parties.

10. Rules of Juvenile Procedure

The Rules of Juvenile Procedure govern the procedure "in the courts of West Virginia having jurisdiction over delinquency and status offense matters."[5] In the case of conflict, these rules trump other West Virginia rules or statutes.[6]

---

5. W. Va. R. Juv. P. 1(a).

6. *Id.*

This comprehensive set of rules address matters such as informing the juvenile of the charges, sentencing the juvenile, and the confidentiality of juvenile records.

C. Family Court Proceedings

1. Rules of Practice and Procedure for Family Court

The Rules of Practice and Procedure for Family Court govern all proceedings in the family courts of West Virginia, with the exception of domestic violence civil proceedings. In the case of conflict, these rules trump other West Virginia rules or statutes. This comprehensive set of rules covers family law issues such as support orders, financial disclosures, temporary relief provisions, testimony of children, and telephonic and videoconferencing hearings.

2. Rules of Practice and Procedure for Domestic Violence Civil Proceedings

As noted above, there are special rules for domestic violence proceedings, whether they are held in West Virginia circuit courts, family courts, or magistrate courts.

D. Magistrate Court Proceedings

1. Rules of Civil Procedure for Magistrate Courts of West Virginia

The Rules of Civil Procedure for Magistrate Courts govern the procedure for civil cases brought in West Virginia magistrate courts. These rules supplement Chapter 50 of the West Virginia Code, which also governs magistrate courts. These rules address matters such as the form of pleadings and motions, which parties may be joined to a proceeding, the scope and limits of discovery, requirements if a trial is heard by a jury, the entry of judgment, and appeals to circuit court.

2. Rules of Criminal Procedure for Magistrate Courts of West Virginia

Similarly, the Rules of Criminal Procedure for Magistrate Courts of West Virginia govern the procedure for criminal cases brought in West Virginia magistrate courts. These rules supplement Chapter 50 of the West Virginia Code, which also governs magistrate courts, and Chapter 62, which governs criminal procedure. These rules address arrest warrants, failure for a party to appear, and citations for traffic offenses and other similar misdemeanors.

III. Federal Court Rules

Like West Virginia state courts, federal courts create their own sets of rules governing the way business is conducted in the federal system. Examples include the Federal Rules of Appellate Procedure, Federal Rules of Civil Procedure, the Federal Rules of Criminal Procedure, and the Federal Rules of Evidence. These rules uniformly apply in all federal courts.

In addition to these rules, there are other local rules applicable to only certain federal courts, such as the United States Supreme Court or the federal bankruptcy courts. In addition, all lower federal courts, including the Northern and Southern District Courts of West Virginia, promulgate their own procedural rules. Local rules can supplement national rules, but they must be consistent.

In addition to being available on numerous websites, these rules also appear at the end of the print volumes of the West Virginia Code. They also are included in volumes of the *United States Code Annotated* and the *United States Code Service.*

IV. Ethics

A. Introduction

Lawyers and judges are not above the law — they must comply with many rules that govern the practice of law. Researchers seeking information related to legal ethics and professional responsibility must consult multiple authorities, as there are a variety of sources on the subject. These authorities are discussed next.

B. West Virginia Rules of Professional Conduct

The West Virginia Rules of Professional Conduct describe the duties and responsibilities of lawyers practicing in the state. A lawyer practicing in the state must follow these rules or face sanctions, lawsuits, or disbarment.

These rules are published in the Michie's and West versions of the West Virginia Code, with annotations that provide comments and links to relevant case law.

The Preamble to West Virginia's Rules of Professional Conduct stresses that lawyers should be competent, prompt, and diligent; uphold communications with a client; and maintain client confidentiality.[7] The rules describe proper conduct as well as conduct that will result in disciplinary action against the lawyer. The rules govern lawyers' conduct both in representing clients (i.e., a lawyer must represent a client competently) and in their personal lives (i.e., a criminal conviction of a lawyer reflects adversely on a lawyer's honesty and therefore violates the rules).[8]

Failure to follow the West Virginia Rules of Professional Conduct may result in discipline by the Lawyer Disciplinary Board and the Office of Disciplinary Counsel. The Supreme Court of Appeals of West Virginia is the final arbiter in legal disciplinary cases and may sanction or disbar a lawyer for serious or multiple ethics violations.

Questions about the meaning or application of a particular rule can be directed to the Office of Disciplinary Counsel. In addition, the West Virginia State Bar website provides links to advisory opinions issued by the Unlawful Practice of Law Committee.[9]

C. West Virginia Standards of Professional Conduct

The West Virginia Office of Disciplinary Counsel adopted the West Virginia Standards of Professional Conduct in 1997.[10] These rules were enacted to address a loss of common courtesy and to ensure that "judges and lawyers ... revive valuable traditions that may be lost."[11] These standards are not binding, and lawyers cannot be sanctioned for failure to follow them. However, these standards provide professional guidance for lawyers with respect to conduct toward other counsel and the courts.

D. Legal Ethics Opinions

The West Virginia Office of Disciplinary Counsel's website contains links to legal ethics opinions issued by the state's Lawyer Disciplinary Board. The Lawyer Disciplinary Board issues advisory opinions regarding the ethical pro-

---

7. W. Va. R. Prof'l Conduct pmbl.
8. W. Va. R. Prof'l Conduct 1.1, 8.4.
9. The address is https://www.wvbar.org/public-information/advisory-opinions/.
10. W. Va. R. Prof'l Conduct, *available at* http://www.wvodc.org/sopc.htm.
11. *Id.*

priety of attorney conduct. Opinions are searchable chronologically or by subject matter.[12]

E. Model Rules of Professional Responsibility

The American Bar Association (ABA) *Model Rules of Professional Conduct* were adopted by the ABA House of Delegates in 1983. They serve as the model for the ethics rules of most states.

V. Rules Governing Lawyers and Judges

The West Virginia Supreme Court of Appeals promulgates rules that govern the practice of law. Specifically, these rules address the requirements for admission to the West Virginia Bar, the procedure for lawyer discipline, and rules governing judicial conduct and judicial disciplinary proceedings.

A. Rules for Admission to the Practice of Law

These rules govern the process for admission to the practice of law in West Virginia. They describe the testing requirements as well as the requirement for good moral character; both are required for admission to practice law.[13]

B. Rules of Lawyer Disciplinary Procedure

The Rules of Lawyer Disciplinary Procedure outline the structure of the Lawyer Disciplinary Board, which has the authority to discipline lawyers who violate the Rules of Professional Conduct. These rules also govern the procedure for lawyer discipline.

C. Code of Judicial Conduct

The Code of Judicial Conduct establishes ethical conduct standards for West Virginia judges. It consists of broad statements called Canons, specific rules set forth in Sections under each Canon, an Application Canon, Commentary, and a Terminology Section. The text of the Canons, the Sections, and the Terminology is authoritative. The Commentary provides guidance on the purpose

---

12. Legal Ethics Opinions may be accessed at http://www.wvodc.org/leo.html.
13. W. Va. R. Admission Prac. Law 2.0, 3.2, 4.2.

and meaning of the Canons and Sections, but is not intended to be a statement of additional rules.

D. Rules of Judicial Disciplinary Procedure

The Rules of Judicial Disciplinary Procedure outline the mechanisms of the Judicial Investigation Commission, the Judicial Hearing Board, and the Office of Disciplinary Counsel. These groups have the authority to discipline judges who violate the Code of Judicial Conduct.

VI. Additional Resources

ABA Links to Professional Responsibility Rules for Every State
http://www.americanbar.org/groups/professional_responsibility/resources/links_of_interest.html

Office of Disciplinary Counsel Legal Ethics Opinions
http://www.wvodc.org/leo.html

Rules of Civil Procedure for Magistrate Courts of West Virginia
http://www.courtswv.gov/legal-community/court-rules/Magistrate/mag-civil.html

Rules of Criminal Procedure for Magistrate Courts of West Virginia
http://www.courtswv.gov/legal-community/court-rules/Magistrate/mag-criminal.html

United States Courts Links to Federal Rules
http://www.uscourts.gov/RulesAndPolicies/rules/current-rules.aspx

United States Courts Links to Local Federal Court Rules
http://www.uscourts.gov/Court_Locator/CourtWebsites.aspx

West Virginia Code of Judicial Conduct
http://www.courtswv.gov/legal-community/court-rules/judicial-conduct/judicial-conduct.html

West Virginia Judiciary Website List of Court Rules
http://www.courtswv.gov/legal-community/court-rules.html

West Virginia Rules for Admission to the Practice of Law
http://www.courtswv.gov/legal-community/rules-for-admission.html#admission-2

West Virginia Rules Governing Post-Conviction Habeas Corpus Proceedings
http://www.courtswv.gov/legal-community/court-rules/habeas/habeas-contents.html#habeas-1

West Virginia Rules of Appellate Procedure
    http://www.courtswv.gov/legal-community/court-rules/appellate-
    procedure/contents.html

West Virginia Rules of Civil Procedure
    http://www.courtswv.gov/legal-community/court-rules/civil-procedure/
    contents.html

West Virginia Rules of Criminal Procedure
    http://www.courtswv.gov/legal-community/court-rules/criminal-
    procedure/contents.html

West Virginia Rules of Evidence
    http://www.courtswv.gov/legal-community/court-rules/evidence-rules/
    contents.html

West Virginia Rules of Lawyer Disciplinary Procedure
    http://www.wvodc.org/roldp.htm

West Virginia Rules of Judicial Disciplinary Procedure
    http://www.courtswv.gov/legal-community/court-rules/judicial-discipl-
    inary/judicial-contents.html

West Virginia Rules of Juvenile Procedure
    http://www.courtswv.gov/legal-community/court-rules/juvenile-
    procedure/juvenile-contents.html

West Virginia Rules of Practice and Procedure for Domestic Violence Civil
Proceedings
    http://www.courtswv.gov/legal-community/court-rules/domestic-
    violence/domestic-contents.html

West Virginia Rules of Practice and Procedure for Family Court
    http://www.courtswv.gov/legal-community/court-rules/Family-Court/
    contents.html

West Virginia Rules of Practice and Procedure for Minor Guardianship
Proceedings
    http://www.courtswv.gov/legal-community/court-rules/MinorGuardian/
    contents.html

West Virginia Rules of Procedure for Administrative Appeals
    http://www.courtswv.gov/legal-community/court-rules/admin-appeals/
    contents.html

West Virginia Rules of Procedure for Child Abuse and Neglect Proceedings
    http://www.courtswv.gov/legal-community/court-rules/child-abuse/child-
    abuse-contents.html

West Virginia Rules of Professional Conduct
    http://www.wvodc.org/ropc.htm

West Virginia Standards of Professional Conduct
    http://www.wvodc.org/sopc.htm

West Virginia Trial Court Rules
    http://www.courtswv.gov/legal-community/court-rules/trial-court/
    contents.html

Chapter Eight

Practice Guides and Professional Materials Research

I. Introduction

Newer researchers may not be familiar with practice guides and professional materials, but these resources provide some of the most up-to-date information on local and cutting-edge topics. Attorneys, bar associations, continuing education providers, and private entities produce these materials to assist practitioners directly in the practice of law. For example, the West Virginia State Bar partners with a publishing company to produce *The West Virginia Lawyer*, a quarterly magazine intended to help practitioners stay abreast of the latest legal developments. Articles contained in *The West Virginia Lawyer* fall under the umbrella of "practice materials" that are not typically cited, but can provide valuable education to legal professionals. Because West Virginia is a small state with a small bar, the library of practice guides and professional materials is somewhat limited. However, West Virginia attorneys have found success with the resources highlighted in this chapter.

II. West Virginia Continuing Legal Education

West Virginia Continuing Legal Education, housed in WVU College of Law, became an official affiliate of West Virginia University in 2016. Providing a hearty series of live and online seminars as well as recorded seminars viewable on personal devices, the office produces written materials to accompany each seminar. These materials are particularly helpful for conducting research on local and new topics that may not appear in more traditional secondary sources or even searches in commercial databases. For example, information regarding two current topics presented by the West Virginia CLE office—"New Developments in The Shale Gas Play" and "Ethical Duties That Cybersecurity & Mobile Practice Demand"— might not appear in Westlaw or Lexis searches. Thus, these materials can be particularly useful for emerging areas of law. In addition, the office provides current information on legal areas that are in flux, such as "Immigration Policies Every Lawyer Should Know." Complete libraries of all of the written materials produced by the office for an entire calendar year are available at a reasonable cost.

III. Form Books

Form books, which contain fill-in-the-blank templates to assist lawyers in drafting documents, can keep newer lawyers from having to reinvent the wheel. While each document you draft will typically contain some nuances not included in a form document, form books can be an excellent starting place.

For West Virginia practitioners, the forms contained in *Michie's State Court Rules* have proven to be particularly valuable. Found at the end of the state code volumes (both Michie's and West), these forms can help you with a variety of filings, including summons, complaints, motions to dismiss, answers, motions for production, and subpoenas.

Forms specific to West Virginia filing can be found in the following sets of rules: the Rules of Practice and Procedure for Family Court, the West Virginia Rules of Procedure for Administrative Appeals, the West Virginia Rules of Criminal Procedure for Magistrate Court, the West Virginia Rules of Appellate Procedure, and the West Virginia Post-Conviction Habeas Corpus Proceedings.

In addition, the West Virginia judiciary offers pro se guides and forms through its website.[1] Under the "public resources" menu, the judiciary provides a wide range of commonly used forms, such as Family Court forms (parenting plans, petitions for support, etc.), Forms for Expungement of Criminal Records, and Fee Waiver forms for use in Magistrate, Circuit, and Family Court. The site also includes valuable information for the general public, including court information by county and FAQs on jury duty.

For federal practitioners, national court forms that can be used in all federal courts are available on the US Courts website.[2] The database is wide-ranging, including forms for everything from drafting a Subpoena to Testify at a Deposition in a Civil Action to a fill-in-the-blank "Defendant's Answer to The

---

1. The address is http://www.courtswv.gov/public-resources.
2. The address is http://www.uscourts.gov/services-forms/forms.

Complaint." Each federal court also maintains its own local court forms, which can be found using the "Court Locator" tab on the same website.

Finally, WestlawNext and Lexis Advance have both created new product lines that offer both forms and other practice-related enhancements. West-lawNext launched Practical Law, which creates and maintains a wide range of practice resources designed to give attorneys a better starting point for their research. The tool not only features a "Standard Documents and Clauses" section with practical drafting and negotiating guidance, but also allows these materials to be downloaded and saved in Microsoft Word for easy editing. Practical Law produces a monthly companion to its online service via Practical Law the Journal, which is offered in two editions—Business & Transactions and Litigation.

Along the same lines, Lexis Advance has developed Lexis Practice Advisor, a tool designed for transactional lawyers. Located in the Lexis Advance Research Menu, Lexis Practice Advisor offers practice notes, forms, clauses, checklists, and drafting notes written by leading practitioners. For law students and newer attorneys, the forms and checklists will jumpstart drafting projects and improve efficiency. Some of the specific topics covered include Capital Markets & Corporate Governance, Commercial Transactions, Corporate and M&A, and Finance.

IV. West Virginia Treatises

West Virginia practitioners heavily rely on a collection of "handbooks" produced specifically for navigating the West Virginia court system. These resources are a cross between a treatise and a professional guidebook, offering valuable background information as well as some forms.

Table 8-1 lists four of the most popular professional resources for West Virginia lawyers.

Newer practitioners rave about the *West Virginia Practice Handbook*, a practical guide created by the Young Lawyers Section of the West Virginia State Bar. Designed for newer lawyers, the book is not intended to supplant your own legal research, but it provides an excellent start. Topics run the gamut from West Virginia Magistrate Court Practice to a state-specific primer on Driving Under the Influence. The Handbook also includes some forms and is free on the Young Lawyers' website.[3]

---

3. The address is http://www.wvyounglawyers.com/.

Table 8-1. Popular Professional Resources for West Virginia Lawyers

Handbook and Author	Brief Description
Handbook of West Virginia Criminal Procedure (Cleckley)	A comprehensive analysis of the constitutional principles and practical considerations commonly confronted by prosecutors and defense counsel in West Virginia criminal trials
Handbook on Evidence for West Virginia Lawyers (Cleckley)	An up-to-date analysis of the law of evidence as it affects West Virginia lawyers
Litigation Handbook on West Virginia Rules of Civil Procedure (Cleckley, Davis, Palmer)	A handbook helpful for researchers looking to gain a fundamental understanding of the application of the West Virginia Rules of Civil Procedure
Trial Handbook for West Virginia Lawyers (Meyer)	An analysis of questions of law that frequently arise during both criminal and civil trials

In addition, practitioners sometimes consult West Virginia-specific materials created by the National Business Institute, a major provider of continuing legal education.

V. Citing Professional Materials

Details on citation forms for professional materials appear in Chapter 10, but here are several examples for quick reference:

- Elliott Manning, *Partnerships — Current and Liquidating Distributions; Death or Retirement of a Partner*, 716-2nd Tax Mgmt. (BNA) U.S. Income, at A-2 (Sept. 24, 2009)

- 1 Franklin D. Cleckley, *Handbook on Evidence for West Virginia Lawyers* § 2-1(E)(2) (4th ed. 2000)

- Stephen P. Meyer, *Trial Handbook for West Virginia Lawyers* § 25:19 (2012)

VI. Additional Resources

National Business Institute
Click the "Seminars" tab and then select West Virginia to see the full list of credit-eligible courses
http://www.nbi-sems.com

West Virginia Continuing Legal Education
Main Website:
   http://wvcle.wvu.edu

West Virginia Judiciary Website
Court Forms
   http://www.courtswv.gov/legal-community/court-forms.html
Court Rules
   http://www.courtswv.gov/legal-community/court-rules.html

National Federal Courts Form Database
   http://www.uscourts.gov/services-forms/forms
Public Resources
   http://www.courtswv.gov/public-resources

West Virginia Practice Handbook
   http://www.wvyounglawyers.com/handbook.html

The West Virginia Lawyer
   https://www.wvbar.org/news/publications/wv-lawyer-magazine/

Chapter Nine

Conducting Research Online

I. Introduction

In the past few years, some have argued that because so many legal resources are now available on the Internet, legal research has become "simple." But those who teach and study legal research have spotted a different trend: legal research via the Internet can be a precarious proposition. Internet sources need to be evaluated carefully, and because there is not yet a comprehensive and free American digital law library, researchers must often master multiple platforms to access just the primary legal resources they need. Moreover, inexperienced researchers may retrieve documents from the Internet but not fully understand each authority's weight — or lack thereof.

The digital revolution has indeed created greater public access to legal information, and the future for legal researchers is full of exciting possibilities. But in this transitional phase, when anyone can post information without attention to accuracy, the legal researcher needs to proceed cautiously. It takes time to become proficient in Internet-based legal research. In this chapter, you will learn about considerations to make before engaging in online research, how to prepare for successful Internet-based legal research, and which sites currently offer the premiere and most accurate legal content.

II. Considerations for Conducting Research on the Internet

While a cruise through cyberspace may seem like the natural starting place for any legal research project, there are a few considerations to take into account before consulting your favorite search engine. First, think about your client's research budget. This may seem counterintuitive, as Internet legal research is "free" in a sense, but as most lawyers recognize, time is money. If you are not yet proficient with Internet-based research or if the information you are seeking is quickly accessible on Lexis or Westlaw, those options could be more cost-effective than a directionless Google search.

Also, consider the superiority of print sources for some types of research. Particularly if you are researching a local topic, a book produced by a continuing legal education series may have the information you need in a handy single volume. Ultimately, this could save your client money because you will find the sources you need so much more efficiently.

The type of research needed (for example, factual versus legal) also may influence your research path. Some basic factual information can be retrieved with a simple Google or Whitepages[1] search; these types of questions lend themselves to Internet research. However, many popular secondary sources are much harder to come by via the Internet because of copyright issues. If those sources answer your questions, a fee-based search may be more cost-effective in the long run, as your hourly rate scouring the Internet could exceed the cost of an efficient Lexis or Westlaw search.

III. Preparing for Successful Internet-Based Research

To become a successful Internet-based legal researcher, you first need to learn about which sources are freely available. Federal law is often easier to access online than state law; you may struggle to find any online information for some narrow local issues. For example, some localities have not posted vital legal information, such as local building codes, online. Fee-based searches or even book-based research may make more sense in those situations.

To become a proficient Internet researcher, locate your own "favorite" research websites, bookmark them, and return to them often. As with any skill, the more you practice, the more comfortable and agile you will become.

IV. Suggested Online Research Sites

An increasing amount of legal information becomes available on the Internet each day. The challenge for the legal researcher is to find reliable sites that are

---

1. The address is http://www.whitepages.com; this website provides the equivalent of an online telephone book.

easy to navigate. The sites described in the remainder of this chapter are generally considered to be some of the best for legal research.

A. General Legal Research Sites

West Virginia University College of Law Library (http://law.wvu.edu/library): The George R. Farmer, Jr. Law Library is the largest public law library in West Virginia. Its website offers links to many relevant Internet sources and subscription services available to the public.

FindLaw (http://lp.findlaw.com): Published by the same company that brings you Westlaw, the free service FindLaw provides links to online legal resources for legal professionals. You can find state and federal primary legal material, as well as legal material from other countries. FindLaw's West Virginia page provides links to online versions of the West Virginia Code, the West Virginia Code of State Rules, as well as federal and state court opinions.[2]

Justia (http://www.justia.com): Justia focuses on making primary legal materials and community resources free and easy to find on the Internet. The site provides free access to a variety of legal information, some arranged by practice specialty. On the West Virginia state page, researchers can find statistical information about the state as well as general state legal resources.[3]

Law Library of Congress (http://www.loc.gov/law): While the Law Library of Congress pages could be classified as a governmental website, the legal information available through the site is so comprehensive that it could just as easily be viewed as a top general legal search site. In addition to the vast amount of legislative information provided, this site offers links to primary federal and state legal resources, as well as in-depth foreign law materials. The "Ask a Librarian" page provides another useful tool, allowing the public to submit questions to experts.

Legal Information Institute (http://www.law.cornell.edu): Cornell was an early adopter in providing legal research via the Internet; its web resources are well respected and touted for accuracy. The Legal Information Institute's online collection is extensive, including Supreme Court decisions, the U.S. Code, the U.S. Constitution, the Federal Rules of Evidence and Civil Procedure, as well as links to state resources. The "Legal Encyclopedia" tab directs readers to sections of Wex, the Institute's collaboratively-edited legal dictionary and encyclopedia.

---

2. The address is http://www.findlaw.com/casecode/west-virginia.html.
3. The address is http://www.justia.com/us-states/west-virginia.

Public Library of Law (http://www.plol.org): The Public Library of Law was created by the makers of Fastcase, and includes ads for fee-based content through the Fastcase service. This site provides free access to primary sources in U.S. law, including federal and state cases, statutes, regulations, and constitutions. The site also offers low-cost legal forms.

WashLaw Legal Research on the Web (http://www.washlaw.edu): This site provides a large and diverse collection of web links to legal material, maintained by the Washburn School of Law. The major categories of information include federal government links, state links, and foreign and international government links.

B. Government Information

Government websites provide legal information for free. The following sites provide federal government information as well as starting points for locating state law.

1. Federal Courts

Federal Court Locator (http://www.uscourts.gov/court_locator.aspx): The Administrative Office of the U.S. Courts provides links to all available federal court websites. Simply click in the Fourth Circuit area on the United States map to retrieve a list of courts within the circuit, many with web links provided. Also, many of the courts listed provide at least a selection of their opinions online for free.

Supreme Court Official Website (http://www.supremecourt.gov): The Supreme Court's official website includes Court calendars and schedules, background information about the Court and justices, rules, bar admissions information, case handling guides, and general public information. The site also provides slip opinions for the current term, PDF copies of the bound *United States Reports* dating back to 1991, and advance sheets (with links to opinions) for previous terms not yet published in a bound volume.

USA.gov (https://www.usa.gov): Billed as an online guide to government information and services, this site has a specialized search function that returns results from only government web pages for more accurate results. The site, which provides helpful links to government contacts by topic, also offers the assistance of an information specialist through a toll-free line, webchat or email contact form.

2. State Courts

National Center for State Courts (NCSC) (http://www.ncsc.org): Many courts now provide their opinions online in PDF form. Bookmark the NCSC directory of State Court Web Sites, as it provides an excellent starting place for state court research.[4]

LLMC Digital (http://www.llmc-digital.org): LLMC Digital, a consortium of academic law libraries, is a leader in digitizing state court information, particularly of a historical nature. This resource is very useful if you are searching for older legal materials. Contact the West Virginia University College of Law Library for subscriber information.

C. Legislation and Regulations

1. Federal

Law Library of Congress (http://www.loc.gov/law/): After many years of operating under the THOMAS banner, the Law Library of Congress has migrated Congressional materials to a revamped legislative site known as congress.gov. The site is a one-stop shop for federal legislative material. The site provides easy access to new public laws, pending bills, status of bills, committee reports, and hearings. It offers the full text of legislation from 1973 (93rd Congress) to present, with bill summary/status information available for the same period.

Office of the Law Revision Counsel (http://uscode.house.gov): This office within the U.S. House of Representatives offers several options for accessing the current and historical editions of the official United States Code in both HTML and PDF formats.

Federal Digital System (http://www.gpo.gov/fdsys): This Government Printing Office site offers free access to official publications from all three branches of the federal government. It provides full-text access to the Code of Federal Regulations (dating back to 1996), the *Federal Register* (dating back to 1970), the *Congressional Record* (dating back to 1994), and other government documents from the U.S. Government Printing Office.

Federal Administrative Agency Actions (http://guides.lib.virginia.edu/administrative_decisions): The University of Virginia Library has compiled an interesting list of administrative agency actions not covered in the Code of

---

4. The address is http://www.ncsc.org/Information-and-Resources/Browse-by-State/State-Court-Websites.aspx.

Federal Regulations or *Federal Register*. While incomplete, it can be searched by agency or by subject.

USA.gov (http://www.usa.gov): The site USA.gov provides access to local, state, and federal government resources. The most helpful feature for legal researchers is the alphabetic list of government agencies and departments, with links to their websites.

2. State

The content of the following websites has been explored in depth in other chapters. According to law librarians at West Virginia University College of Law, the most popular legal research websites for West Virginia materials are the following:

- West Virginia State Bar: https://www.wvbar.org
- West Virginia Secretary of State: http://sos.wv.gov/Pages/default.aspx
- West Virginia Judiciary: http://www.courtswv.gov
- West Virginia Legislature: http://www.wvlegislature.gov

D. Legal Periodicals

While secondary sources are harder to come by via the Internet, an increasing amount of legal scholarship is now available. The sites below provide access to many full-text online legal journals, which can provide solid leads to primary law sources, particularly on cutting-edge topics.

The American Bar Association's Legal Technology Resource Center Journal Search (http://www.americanbar.org/groups/departments_offices/legal_technology _resources/resources/free_journal_search.html): Powered by Google Custom Search Engines, this resource allows you to search the full text of articles from more than 400 law journals.

Google Scholar (http://scholar.google.com): Popular with students, Google Scholar allows researchers to find law review articles, or at least abstracts of those articles, through a simple search for "Articles" on the Scholar homepage. Once you have identified relevant articles, HeinOnline (discussed below) may provide full-text access, especially with older articles.

HeinOnline (http://home.heinonline.org): HeinOnline provides full-text access to hundreds of law reviews and journals, including many of the older editions not freely available through the Internet. Contact the West Virginia University College of Law Library for access questions.

Social Science Research Network (http://www.ssrn.com): This site provides abstracts and PDFs for thousands of scholarly papers, including working papers and pre-publication versions of legal journal articles. This source would be particularly helpful if you are researching a new topic on which very little has been written.

E. Lower-Cost Research Services

Researchers also may be interested in the lower-cost legal research services that have emerged in recent years.

Fastcase (http://www.fastcase.com): Fastcase is an online research service offered by nearly half of the state bar associations to its members, including West Virginia. Fastcase includes fifty state and federal case law databases. Much of the fee-based material can be accessed via links from the free Public Library of Law site, which is maintained by the same company.[5]

V. Enhancements via Commercial Services

While this chapter has offered many suggestions for performing free legal research, the bells and whistles that commercial services provide make them worth considering. For example, legal researchers need an organizational strategy for dealing with the results of online searching, and each of the commercial providers allows researchers to create folders and annotate findings. The time savings could outweigh the financial cost.

In addition, some particularly attractive features available through commercial services include the following:

- **Westlaw Research Recommendations.** Essentially, Westlaw detects legal issue patterns in search results and recommends additional sources to consult.
- **Westlaw Folder Analysis.** This tool is based on the same concept as Research Recommendations, but instead of analyzing searches, this feature scans your folders to identify legal issues, and then suggests additional sources.
- **Westlaw Answers.** Law students can benefit from this tool, which provides specific answers to common legal questions. It also suggests leading cases to back up the answers.
- **Lexis Practice Advisor.** Especially valuable for transactional attorneys and newer lawyers, this tool was created to provide a one-stop resource

---

5. The address is http://www.plol.org.

for a broad range of transactional issues. Less experienced practitioners may especially appreciate the practice and drafting notes crafted by leading transactional attorneys.

Chapter Ten

Legal Citation

I. The Purpose of Citation

Good legal writers rely on authority to bolster assertions made within their arguments. Proper legal citation conveys the source for the authority cited as well as the weight of that source. Whether drafting a brief to the court or a memorandum to a supervising attorney, legal writers must cite authority with care. Proper citation lends both credibility and a professional appearance to a legal writer's work.

At the most basic level, a legal citation provides the name of a source and the published location of that source. With a standard system of legal citation, readers can easily identify, locate, and review your sources. There are four general purposes for legal citation: (1) instructing readers on locating a source, (2) informing readers about the weight and persuasiveness of the source, (3) conveying the type and degree of support provided for a particular proposition, and (4) demonstrating thorough research and support for a writer's position.[1]

This chapter provides guidance about the two most commonly used systems of legal citation in West Virginia: the *Bluebook* and the West Virginia Rules of Appellate Procedure.

II. Citation in West Virginia

As a preliminary note, briefs submitted to trial courts in West Virginia must conform to generally accepted citation form, which means the *Bluebook* in West Virginia.[2] Lower courts in West Virginia do not require parallel citations

---

1. Association of Legal Writing Directors & Coleen M. Barger, ALWD Citation Manual (6th ed. Wolters Kluwer 2017).
2. *See* W. Va. Trial Ct. R. 6.02.

(meaning citations to both state and regional reporters). Instead, writers typically cite only to the regional reporter under the *Bluebook* convention. However, the West Virginia Rules of Appellate Procedure require a parallel citation to any West Virginia case cited in a brief or other submission to the West Virginia Supreme Court.[3]

The sections that follow discuss the proper citation of cases, statutes, and administrative regulations. In addition, the subsequent sections discuss the proper use of signals and common mistakes with respect to legal citation.

A. West Virginia Revised Rules of Appellate Procedure

The West Virginia Revised Rules of Appellate Procedure became effective December 1, 2010. This set of rules contains the first wide-ranging update in several decades. A few nuances are discussed below; consult the complete set of the Revised Rules of Appellate Procedure before submitting documents to the West Virginia Supreme Court.

1. Rule 21(e): Memorandum Decisions

The West Virginia Rules of Appellate Procedure allow litigants to cite memorandum decisions (abbreviated decisions on the merits of a case which do not contain a syllabus) of the West Virginia Supreme Court.[4] The West Virginia Supreme Court may issue memorandum decisions on mature cases. Although West Virginia memorandum decisions are not published in the *West Virginia Reports*, memorandum decisions are available on the West Virginia Supreme Court of Appeals website. Memorandum decisions may be cited in any court or tribunal within the State of West Virginia. To properly cite a memorandum decision, include a parenthetical explanation as follows:

> Example: *Lee v. Amfire, LLC*, No. 15-0941 (W. Va. Supreme Court, August 26, 2016) (memorandum decision)

2. Rules 6 and 38(d): Record on Appeal and General Form and Filing Requirements

When writing to the West Virginia Supreme Court of Appeals, be sure that any material cited in your brief is actually included in the appellate record— rather than just the trial court record.[5] Additionally, place all citations in the

---

3. W. Va. Rev. R. App. P. 38(d).
4. W. Va. Rev. R. App. P. 21(e).
5. *See* W. Va. Rev. R. App. P. 6(b).

body of the document.[6] (Only use footnote citations when citing more than five authorities together, which you should avoid.) When citing cases decided by the West Virginia Supreme Court of Appeals, you must include a parallel citation to the *West Virginia Reports*. If the opinion is per curiam (note that the West Virginia Supreme Court of Appeals stopped issuing per curiam opinions in 2014), you should indicate that in a parenthetical, as follows:

Example: *State v. Flournoy,* 232 W. Va. 175, 751 S.E.2d 280 (2013) (per curiam)

B. The *Bluebook*

Editors of the *Columbia Law Review, Harvard Law Review, University of Pennsylvania Law Review,* and *Yale Law Journal* compile the *Bluebook,* the oldest and most widely known citation manual. This resource includes more than 400 pages with the goal of providing a uniform system of citation. Although largely directed toward citation for law review articles and other scholarly work, the *Bluebook* contains a Bluepages section that covers the basics of legal citation for practicing attorneys. (This section is printed with a light blue overlay for easy detection.) For more complex citation issues, the Bluepages reference supplemental authority in the section that follows the Bluepages, known as the Whitepages.

The Bluepages are located at the front of the *Bluebook.* This section contains a discussion of the differences between law review citation format and citation for court documents and legal memoranda. Most notably, law review citations differ from non-academic citations with respect to font style. Law review articles use small and large caps (while court documents and legal memoranda do not) and have different rules for underlining or italicizing case names.

The *Bluebook* contains a table of contents, quick reference materials on the inside of both covers, and a detailed index. To efficiently use the *Bluebook,* the index is the most complete resource for locating the proper citation rules. To properly use the *Bluebook* or any other system of citation, follow this process:

1. identify the type of source you are citing;
2. locate the appropriate rule via the index (or table of contents);
3. gather the required elements from the source for a proper citation; and
4. assemble those elements according to the rule.

Although you will probably find most of the necessary citation information within one rule, certain citations require you to apply additional rules. When

---

6. W. Va. Rev. R. App. P. 38(d).

assembling a citation, always be aware of technical rules on spacing, italicizing or underlining, and signals preceding the citation.

III. Case Citation

Each full citation to a reported case must include the following information: (1) the case name; (2) the volume of the reporter, the abbreviated name of the reporter, the page the case first appears, and the specific page that supports your statement; (3) the geographic jurisdiction and court where the case was decided; and (4) the year the case was decided. Generally, a full case citation includes the following:

Example: *Benjamin v. Walker*, 786 S.E.2d 200, 201 (W. Va. 2016)

A. Case Name

A proper case citation often excludes certain case name information that will be displayed in the case reporter. Be aware that the citation provided by commercial, electronic databases may not always comply with proper *Bluebook* form. The citation to a case should cite only the first party listed on each side of the case. For individuals, the names used should be each party's surname. In addition, case names should be abbreviated.[7] On the other hand, if referencing a case in a textual sentence, only abbreviate widely recognized acronyms and certain words listed in the citation manual rules.

B. Reporter and Page

Whether viewing a case from an online database or from a print reporter, case citations must be cited with reference to the print reporter. Cases from the West Virginia Supreme Court of Appeals are currently published in the *South Eastern Reporter*, a West reporter. The *South Eastern Reporter* is currently in its second series, which is cited as S.E.2d.

Federal cases decided in federal district courts are reported in the *Federal Supplement*, which is currently in its third series. Federal cases decided by the Fourth Circuit are reported in the *Federal Reporter*, and are abbreviated as F, F.2d, or F.3d depending upon the series of the reporter. Cases decided by the United States Supreme Court are reported in the *United States Reports* (U.S.) or the *Supreme Court Reporter* (S. Ct.).

---

7. *See Bluebook* Rule 10.2.2 and Table T6.

Table 10-1. Federal Courts Sitting in West Virginia

N.D.W. Va.	Northern District of West Virginia
S.D.W. Va.	Southern District of West Virginia
4th Cir.	Fourth Circuit Court of Appeals

The portion of a case citation referencing the reporter takes the following form: (1) the volume of the reporter, (2) the abbreviation for the name of the reporter, and (3) the page on which the case first appears in the reporter. In addition, you should provide a pinpoint citation (commonly referred to as a "pincite"), which is the page number for the exact page on which the material you are citing appears. In a full citation, a pinpoint citation will be expressed with a comma and page number following the citation to the first page on which the case appears. Providing a pinpoint citation enables your reader to quickly locate your cited authority. If you are citing to the first page on which the case appears, still provide a pinpoint citation to that page.

To locate the page number in an online version of a case, look for an asterisk (*) followed by a page number. Make sure that you use the page number that corresponds to the reporter that you are citing, as the page numbers for multiple reporters will be available online. Never cite to the headnotes or other editorial content that precedes the beginning of a case; however, syllabus points in West Virginia cases may be cited.

C. Jurisdiction and Court

In the parenthetical following the case name, reporter, and page number, you must reference the court/jurisdiction of the reported decision. For West Virginia state cases, W. Va. is the proper abbreviation. Because West Virginia has only one appellate court, no additional court abbreviation is necessary to indicate that the West Virginia Supreme Court of Appeals made the decision.

Abbreviations for federal courts sitting in West Virginia are provided in Table 10-1.

D. Date

Within the parenthetical and directly following the court/jurisdiction, list the publishing date of the court's decision. When looking at a case heading, only use the year in which the case was decided. (For the purposes of citation, disregard the date on which the case was argued or other such dates.) Unless citing an unpublished or slip opinion, the year is the only portion of the date included in the citation.

E. Full Citation v. Short Form Citation

When first citing a case, provide a full citation to that authority as discussed above. Due to the lengthiness of full case citations, if at all possible, place full citations outside of your textual sentence in a separate citation sentence. This technique improves the readability of a legal document.

Once you provide a full citation to a case, you may use the short form thereafter. Taking the *Benjamin* case mentioned above, the following examples illustrate the different forms of acceptable citation:

Full Citation: *Benjamin v. Walker*, 786 S.E.2d 200, 201 (W. Va. 2016)

Short Form: *Benjamin*, 786 S.E.2d at 201

Short Form: 786 S.E.2d at 201

Short Form: *Id.* at 201

Short Form: *Id.*

With respect to the "*id.*" citation, use *id.* only when the source cited is the only source referenced in the immediately preceding citation. Although the goal of *id.* is to save space in your writing, economy should not come at the expense of clarity. Make sure to provide page numbers or sections following an *id.* if the cited material appears on a different page than the page(s) referenced in the preceding citation.

F. Syllabus Point Law

In West Virginia Supreme Court opinions, the Court drafts syllabus points that are placed at the beginning of the opinion. Unlike editorial comments, syllabus points have the force of law, and they may be cited as support for a legal proposition. To properly cite syllabus points, add the reference to the syllabus point at the beginning of the citation:

Syl. Pt. 5, *Benjamin v. Walker*, 786 S.E.2d 200, 201 (W. Va. 2016)

IV. Statutes

With respect to statutory citation, the Bluebook prefers citations to a state's official code. However, West Virginia no longer publishes an official Code, but

Table 10-2. West Virginia Statutory Citation Form

Bluebook B12.1.2, Table 1	W. Va. Code Ann. § X-X-X (LexisNexis year)

instead relies on commercial publishers. Because these versions are annotated, the Bluebook requires a reference to that format. Generally, the proper citation to a West Virginia statute includes reference to the chapter, article, and section, as shown in Table 10-2, as well as a parenthetical description of the publisher and year of publication.

Because West Virginia no longer publishes an official code, the parenthetical portion of the citation must include a reference to the commercial publisher. The preference is to cite from a bound (book) version of the Code. The parenthetical should include a reference to the publisher and the date on the spine of the book. If a portion of the statute is found in the supplement (pocket part), the parenthetical depends upon whether all or a portion of the statute appears in the supplement. If the entirety of the cited statute appears in the supplement, the parenthetical should read as follows:

(LexisNexis Supp. 2016)

If the cited portion of the statute appears in both the bound volume and the supplement, the parenthetical should read as follows:

(LexisNexis 2012 & Supp. 2016)

If you are citing a version of the Code found online through a commercial database, the parenthetical includes the name of the publisher followed by the date of the most recent updates to the electronic database version of the Code. The parenthetical would read as follows:

(West 2016) or (LexisNexis 2016)

Remember, unless local rules state otherwise, only academics adhering to law review format would use small and large caps for citations to the West Virginia Code.

V. Rules and Regulations

The West Virginia Secretary of State's office currently posts unofficial copies of all administrative rules and regulations on the Secretary of State's website. The official copies of the Code of State Rules are stamped by the West Virginia Secretary of State and stored in the Secretary of State's office. Generally, ad-

Table 10-3. Administrative Law Citation in West Virginia

Bluebook T1.3	W. Va. Code R. § X-X-X (year)

ministrative rules are cited much like statutes, and require a reference to the title, series, and section, as shown in Table 10-3.

VI. Signals

Signals can introduce a citation sentence and are typically used when the citation does not directly support the proposition provided. For instance, a signal may be used to direct your reader to authority that indirectly supports your proposition or that directly contradicts your proposition. Signals enable you to convey useful information to your reader, and when paired with explanatory parentheticals, signals can help conserve words and space used to convey the same idea in textual sentences. Signals must be italicized and must be ordered within a citation sentence according to each citation system's rules.[8] Practitioners often exclude signals because their propositions are directly supported by the authority cited, and thus, no signal is necessary.

>
> Example: A ski area operator has no duty and is not liable for injuries resulting from "inherent risks essentially impossible for the ski area operator to eliminate, even with 'reasonable' maintenance." *Pinson v. Canaan Valley Resorts, Inc.*, 473 S.E.2d 151, 155 (W. Va. 1996) (citing *Lewis v. Canaan Valley Resorts, Inc.*, 408 S.E.2d 634, 643 n.12 (W. Va. 1991)); *see also* W. Va. Code Ann. § 20-3A-3(8) (LexisNexis 2012) (excusing ski area operators from liability for injuries arising out of enumerated inherent risks).

VII. Common Mistakes

Due to slight differences in citation between states and between style manuals, certain mistakes commonly arise. Here are some reminders to help you avoid common mistakes that occur when citing to courts in West Virginia or

---

8. *See Bluebook* at B3 and R1.2.

Table 10-4. Common Mistakes

Abbreviating West Virginia	When abbreviation W. Va., place a space between "W." and "Va."
Id.	Italicize or underline the period following *id.*
Italicizing and Underlining	Do not italicize or underline: (1) the comma following a case name or (2) the space between a signal and a citation.
Spacing and Font	Pay particular attention to the proper spacing and font of citations to avoid common mistakes.
State Rules	Cite West Virginia Rules of Civil Procedure as W. Va. R. Civ. P. Cite West Virginia Rules of Evidence as WVRE
Syllabus Points	Syllabus Points are part of a judicial opinion and may be cited; headnotes are not part of the judicial opinion and may not be cited.

when citing West Virginia sources. Table 10-4 outlines common mistakes and citation manual nuances.

VIII. Conclusion

By using proper citation, you allow readers to efficiently identify and locate sources that support your argument. Although the *Bluebook* is lengthy, the index and table of contents simplify the citation process. For complex citations not clearly addressed in the *Bluebook*, provide a citation most analogous to the citation for a similar source. Always remember that the overriding purpose of citation is to provide your reader with sufficient information to unambiguously identify and locate the source being cited.

IX. Additional Resources

The Bluebook: A Uniform System of Citation (Columbia Law Review Ass'n et al. eds., 20th ed. 2015).

West Virginia Revised Rules of Appellate Procedure
http://www.courtswv.gov/legal-community/court-rules/appellate-procedure/pdfs/Revised-Rules-of-Appellate-Procedure-FINAL.pdf

West Virginia Secretary of State — Code of State Rules
http://apps.sos.wv.gov/adlaw/csr

West Virginia Supreme Court Memorandum Decisions
http://www.courtswv.gov/supreme-court/opinions.html

West Virginia Trial Court Rules
http://www.courtswv.gov/legal-community/court-rules/trial-court/contents.html

About the Author

Hollee Schwartz Temple is a journalist-turned-lawyer-turned-professor at West Virginia University College of Law. After graduating with a combined bachelor's and master's degree from Northwestern University's Medill School of Journalism, Professor Temple attended Duke University School of Law. She graduated in 1999 and worked as a litigation associate at a large Pittsburgh law firm until she joined the WVU faculty in 2003. She teaches legal research and writing courses and also has directed the College's Legal Analysis, Research & Writing program.

An active scholar and speaker, Professor Temple wrote a regular work/life balance column for the *American Bar Association Journal*, and has been published in newspapers, national law reviews and legal writing publications. She is co-author of *Good Enough Is the New Perfect: Finding Happiness and Success in Modern Motherhood* (Harlequin Nonfiction, 2011). She has presented at many legal writing conferences, and also traveled the country providing keynote addresses on work/life balance for a wide variety of groups—from law firms to women's networks to university conferences.

Index